LAND REVENUE IN INDIA
Historical Studies

Edited by

RAM SHARAN SHARMA

MOTILAL BANARSIDASS PUBLISHERS
PRIVATE LIMITED • DELHI

Reprint : Delhi, 2017
First Edition : 1971

ISBN : 978-81-208-4102-4

Motilal Banarsidass
41 U.A., Bungalow Road, Jawahar Nagar, Delhi 110 007
8 Mahalaxmi Chamber, 22 Bhulabhai Desai Road, Mumbai 400 026
203 Royapettah High Road, Mylapore, Chennai 600 004
236, 9th Main III Block, Jayanagar, Bengaluru 560 011
8 Camac Street, Kolkata 700 017
Ashok Rajpath, Patna 800 004
Chowk, Varanasi 221 001

MLBD Cataloging-in-Publication Data
Land Revenue in India
Edited by DR. RAM SHARAN SHARMA
ISBN : 978-81-208-4102-4
Includes Glossary and Index
I. History II. Economics III. Land Revenue
IV. Sharma, Ram Sharan

Printed in India
by RP Jain at NAB Printing Unit,
A-44, Naraina Industrial Area, Phase I, New Delhi–110028
and published by JP Jain for Motilal Banarsidass Publishers (P) Ltd,
41 U.A. Bungalow Road, Jawahar Nagar, Delhi-110007

PREFACE

The present essays on land revenue system were read and discussed in a local seminar held in the Department of History, Patna University, in 1965. They cover a large span of Indian history and have also something to say on the tribal land system. The first two essays analyse and explain the ground taxes from about B.C. 200 to A.D. 1200, and a comparison between the two shows that several additional taxes appeared in early medieval north India. The third essay deals with the mode of assessment, medium of payment and the method of collection in Mughal times. The discussion on assignments initiated by it is continued in the fourth, which examines the ideas and circumstances leading to the introduction of Permanent Settlement. The peculiarities of the tribal land system in South Bihar are brought out in two essays. They show how the large-scale introduction of ideas of private property in land by non-tribal land-hungry immigrants undermined the existing tribal practices and gave rise to social tensions, political unrest and peasant revolts, which could not be successfully tackled by piecemeal agrarian legislation introduced by the British.

A question discussed in the seminar related to the rise in the incidence of taxation. It was thought that there had been a gradual rise in taxes, but this hypothesis will have to be tested in the light of facts and statistics, which are not available till the 17th century. How taxes in kind were collected and stored was also discussed at some length. That there were local granaries to meet local needs seems to be plausible, but archaeology has to discover other granaries besides the Harappan. The differences between 'secular' and 'religious' grants were discussed, and whether medieval assignments were periodical or hereditary, carried usufructuary or proprietary rights, covered the whole country or certain parts was argued in some detail. It is a pity that the report of these discussions could not be included in this publication. But we hope that in spite of this omission the articles might serve as historical introduction to the Indian land revenue system.

In preparing these essays tor press, I have received the help of Dr. Surendra Gopal and of Dr. D. N. Jha who have read the proofs and prepared the glossary. Dr. R. N. Nandi has performed the tedious task of preparing the index and bibliography. All these colleagues deserve my sincere thanks.

Department of History
Patna University
Patna

R. S. Sharma

15 November, 1970

CONTENTS

I

LAND REVENUE IN THE MAURYA AND GUPTA PERIODS

D. N. Jha

Although our sources are eloquent about the principles of taxation, they are less so about the modes of assessment of land revenue. The *Arthaśāstra* is the first early Indian work to give us some idea of it. Thus one of the duties of the *gopa* (officer in charge of 5 or 10 villages) is stated to be to prepare various registers, such as those of boundaries and village fields, uncultivable lands, and of transfers. He is further required to compile what may be called census-lists of dwelling houses, to specify therein whether the houses are taxable or tax-free, and to state the taxes charged upon them severally under the heads of cash payment, unpaid labour, tolls and fines.[1] The *Arthaśāstra*[2] further provides for the deputation of inspectors by the *samāhartā* in the selected villages, where he is to check up and report on the various heads of revenues assessed on the dwelling houses and the remissions granted to them. It, therefore, follows that in Maurya times land revenue and the connected charges were probably assessed upon the individual holding of the villagers.

Land revenue appears to have been normally charged on individual holding in the Maurya period, but collective assessment on whole villages was not unknown. Kauṭilya[3]

1. *AŚ*, II. 35. In the Roman Empire also, the periodical census furnished lists of the living inhabitants with an estimate of their wealth, so that they could be arranged in classes and their tax could be assessed. This census-list distinguished between the various categories of land : fields under cultivation, plantation of vines or of olives, woods and pastures. Moreover, homes and other buildings were also included in the list, together with movables, furniture, slaves, and even cash savings, all this being regarded as an extension of the landed property, since the incidence of the tax was upon the land itself and not upon its possessor (Victor Chapot, *The Roman World*, London, 1928, pp. 95-96).

2. *Ibid*.

3. *Ibid*. ii. 15.

mentions *piṇḍakara* under the heading *rāṣṭra* (country parts). This term is explained by his commentator Bhaṭṭasvāmin as comprising taxes levied from whole villages. Evidently it stood for a lump assessment upon villages as distinguished from principal land tax which was assessed on individual holdings of land.

In post-Maurya and Gupta times *piṇḍakara* or any other term of similar import is not mentioned in our sources, which implies the absence of collective assessment of any tax on an entire village. The older practice of charging revenue on individual holdings, however, seems to have continued in this period. This can be inferred from the Sātavāhana land charters, which record gifts of plots of land in specified villages.[4] The fact that in these instances the granted fields were to be enjoyed by individuals may suggest that to a certain extent the assessment of land revenue was made upon individual holdings.

The land grants of the Gupta period testify more clearly than the earlier ones to assessment on individual holdings of land. The two charters[5] belonging to the region of modern Indore—one of Mahārāja Svāmidāsa (c. A. D. 386-387) and the other of Mahārāja Bhuluṇḍa (c. A.D. 426-427)—record donations of lands in favour of the brāhmaṇas. Since the holdings of individual cultivators were sought to be donated here, it may suggest that villagers were separately assessed for land revenue. Similarly, an undated inscription of the Parivrājaka ruler Hastin[6], who ruled in the Baghelkhand region of central India, records the gift of half of the village of Dhavasandika. At least two other epigraphs of the Parivrājaka Mahārājas refer to a portion of a village or portions of two different villages forming the object of gift.[7] Again, several documents of the Maitrakas, who ruled in the Gujarat-Kathiawad region probably from the fifth century onwards, mention the king's gift of fields (along with the royal dues therefrom) or wells or both, lying in the extremities of specified villages and forming in many cases the holdings (*pratyāya*) of the cultivators whose names are mentioned. Thus in the Goras copper-plates (A.D.

4. *Lüders' List*, nos. 1162, 1163, 1164, 1166, 1167, etc.
5. *EI*, xv, no. 16 (1 & 2).
6. *grāmārddho*, *CII*, iii, no. 29, l. 8.
7. *IA*, viii, pp. 8, 28.

643) of Dhruvasena II a field consisting of three pieces and measuring 100 *pādāvartas* in the village called Bahumūla is granted. The record states that the field lay to the north of the field of Devī. Another field of 100 *pādāvartas*, donated according to the same record, is described as having the *brahmadeya* field of Sthavira in its west and the holding of Kutumbi Kuhuṇḍaka in the north.[8] All this may imply that the villages concerned were not assessed collectively but with references to individual holdings.

A study of the rate of land tax, as prescribed in our sources, reveals that often the quality of land was an important consideration in assessing land revenue. Gautama,[9] who probably belongs to the pre-Maurya period, prescribes three distinct rates, viz., 1/6, 1/8, and 1/10. The commentator Haradatta takes these rates to apply to different types of soil.[10] Kauṭilya mentions an income called *ṣaḍbhaga*, which perhaps refers to land revenue.[11] In another place, the *Arthasāstra* records the expression *dhānyaṣaḍbhāga*, one-sixth of the grain as being taken by the king. This, however, does not mean that Kauṭilya recognises the uniform rate of 1/6 in all cases. Elsewhere[12] he himself states that upland and lowland are to be recorded separately by the *gopa*. While laying down the rules for extraordinary revenue he further contemplates unhusked grain to be assessed at 1/3 or 1/4 of the crop of rich soils which are independent of rain-water, but soils of intermediate and inferior qualities are evidently assigned lower rates.[13] Among the lawgivers of the later period, Manu[14] ordains that a king can take 1/6, 1/8, or 1/12 of the crops. This passage is quoted in the *Vīramitrodaya*, where it is remarked that the option laid down is based on the varying fertility of the soil and the consequent greater or less labour involved in cultivation.[15] Bṛhas-

8. Disalkar, "Some. Unpublished Copper-plates of the rulers of Valabhi," *JBBRAS*, i (N.S.), pp. 51-52; for similar references see *IA*, i, p. 16; vii, p. 70; viii, p. 301.

9. *Gautama*, x. 24.

10. Haradatta on *Gautama*, x. 24.

11. *AS*, ii. 15.

12. *Ibid.* ii. 35.

13. *Ibid.* V. 2.

14. *dhanyānāmaṣṭamo bhāgaḥ saṣṭho dvādasa eva vā.* *Manu*, VII. 130.

15. Vide G. N. Jha, *Notes on Manusmṛti*, pt. 2. p. 466.

pati[16] lays down the rates of 1/10, 1/8 and 1/6 on *khila* land, on the land exposed to the rain-water, and on the crops harvested in the spring season respectively. *Khila* land may be taken as cultivable waste,[17] the cultivation of which may entail more than the usual cost. Similarly, lands exposed to the dangers of rain-water make a rich harvest uncertain, and the crops harvested in the spring season are least subject to risks. Perhaps in view of these considerations Bṛhaspati prescribes three distinct rates of land tax, which are the same as laid down by Gautama.

Land tax may have been assessed at rates in keeping with the varying fertility of the soil, but most authorities prescribe the rate of 1/6. Manu, who has been quoted earlier as advocating three different rates, states at one place that the king who affords no protection and yet receives the sixth part of the produce takes upon himself all the sins of his people.[18] Both Viṣṇu[19] and Nārada[20] mention 1/6 to be the usual rate of land revenue. It is repeatedly stated in the *Sānti Parva* that the king is entitled to 1/6 of the produce. The rate of 1/6 seems to have been so deeply associated with popular sentiment that the king is often known by the appellative *ṣaḍbhāgin*.[21] A similar attitude is reflected in the works of Kālidāsa, who states that the king can claim 1/6 of the produce of land from the people.[22] He further tells us that the ascetics living in the forest pay the sixth part of their penances;[23] and he refers to them as placing 1/6 of the rice collected by them on the bank of the river to be taken by the royal officers.[24] Thus it seems that the rate of 1/6 was perhaps normally prevalent, though of course variations may have been admissible.[25]

16. *Bṛhaspati*, I. 43.
17. Maity, *The Economic Life of Northern India in the Gupta Period*, Calcutta, 1957, p. 24.
18. *Manu*, VII. 308.
19. Viṣṇu, III. 24.
20. *Nārada*, XVIII. 48.
21. *AS*, II, 15; *Viṣṇu*, III. 22; *Nārada* quoted above; *ŚP*, 69. 24, 72. 10.
22. *Raghu.*, II. 66.
23. *Sāk.*, II. 13.
24. *Ibid.* (Nirnayasagar Press), p. 76.
25. Curiously enough the land charters nowhere directly lay down the

Although 1/6 seems to be the theoretically accepted rate, the account of Megasthenes suggests that in spite of the injunctions of Kauṭilya the Mauryan land tax was much higher. Ghoshal has taken Megasthenes' statement as quoted by Diodorus to mean that the cultivators ordinarily paid 1/4 of the produce to the Mauryan state.[26] The relatively high rate of Mauryan land revenue is also attested by the Rumindei pillar inscription of Asoka, which records the royal order that the village Lumbini, by virtue of its being the birth-place of the Buddha, is liable to 1/8 of the bhāga (*aṭṭhabhāgiya*) and exempted from *bali*. Since this concession was made by Aśoka for the holiest place of his faith and since complete remission of the land revenue not thought of in the Maurya period, it seems that land revenue was fixed sufficiently high to make its reduction to the ratio of 1/8 amount to a very great favour.[27] It appears that although in theory Kauṭilya prescribes 1/6 as the normal rate of land tax, in practice the ratio was much higher; and not less than 1/4 if the Greek testimony is accepted. We do not, however, know whether in the post-Maurya and Gupta periods there was a similar discrepancy between theory and practice. It is curious that the contemporary inscriptions do not give any indication of the rate of land tax, although the occurrence of the expression *dharmaṣaḍbhāga* in several Gupta epigraphs may suggest that the rate of 1/6 was in vogue. This may mean that the king's normal grain share was realised at lower rates in Gupta times than in the Mauryan days.

Equally pertinent and no less controversial is the question whether land tax was imposed on the gross income or on the profit of the cultivator. With regard to tax on merchants our sources implicitly indicate an attempt to shift the burden of taxation on the net profit, but the lawgivers nowhere explicitly state that land tax was assessed on the agriculturists' profit. Kullūka explains a passage of Manu quoted above to mean that the king's share is to be estimated on the increase upon the capital employed. Medhātithi and Govinda are concurrent, and Nandana even more clearly states: "In every case, the share is on profit

rate of land tax to be realised from the villagers, although such terms as *aṣṭabhāgika* and *dharmaṣaḍhbāga* give some indirect idea.

26. *HRS*, p. 168.

27. *Ibid.* p. 171.

made after deducting expenses." But as the commentators belong to a later period their interpretation of the Smṛti passages may not apply to the period under study. Among the contemporary sources the *Śānti Parva*[28] broadly recognises the criteria of income and expenditure in determining the king's share, though, strangely enough, other sources do not seem to suggest that land tax was assessed on the cultivator's profit. However, there may have existed a broad recognition of the fact that taxes should fall on the profit and not on the capital, but how far this principle was observed specifically in relation to land tax is largely a matter of speculation.

The main item of land revenue appears to have been the customary royal share of the agricultural produce sometimes known as *bhāga*. As the designation of a specific tax on land, the word *bhāga* first occurs in the *Arthaśāstra*.[29] At one place it is mentioned as an independent term along with *bali*, *kara*, etc., under the heading *rāṣṭra*; at another[30] it forms a part of *ṣaḍbhāga*, which is mentioned with *bali*, *kara*, etc., under the same general heading. Therefore, "*bhāga* undoubtedly means the king's customary share of the produce normally, though not universally, amounting to 1/6th."[31] Kṣīravāmin,[32] the 12th century commentator of the *Amarakośa*, also quotes the view of the *Arthaśāstra* to define *bhāga* as the king's 1/6th share of produce.

Bhāga seems to have been the principal tax on land in later times as well. In the Junagadh inscription of Rudradāman the royal treasury is said to have been filled with *bali*, *śulka* and *bhāga*, and the Sudarśana dam is said to have been built without oppressing the people with *kara*, *viṣṭi* and *praṇaya*.[33] Since the latter three taxes are referred to as oppressive, *bhāga*, which is not mentioned as such, perhaps stands for the main item of land revenue, i.e., king's normal grain-share. The inscriptions of the Gupta period recording grants of land to the brāhmaṇas frequently refer to the donee's exemption from

28. *ŚP*, 120. 9.
29. *AŚ*, II. 6.
30. *Ibid.* II, 15.
31. U.N. Ghoshal, "Some Hindu Fiscal Terms Discussed". *Proceedings of the Fourth Oriental Conference*, II, p. 205.
32. *rājagrāhyaḥ ṣaḍbhāgādiḥ*, Kṣirasvāmin's comm. on *Amar*. II. 8. 28.
33. *EI*, viii, no. 6, l. 14.

bhāgabhogakara[34] among the other levies. Fleet[35] considers the term *bhāgabhoga* to be one expression meaning "enjoyment of taxes or shares." The two words, however, are sometimes used in the reverse order and recorded as *bhogabhāga.*[36] If we construe this term in the same manner as Fleet does the first, it would mean "share of the enjoyment." But really speaking, this term is a compound formed by two independent words, *bhoga* and *bhāga*, and hence it indicates two separate taxes. Therefore Sircar's[37] explanation of the *bhāga* of inscriptions as the royal share of the produce may be nearer the truth.

Another fiscal expression, *bali*, occurs in early Indian sources. It is the oldest Indo-Aryan term for the royal revenue. In the *Ṛgveda* it is the king's due both from his subjects and from conquered kings.[38] Macdonnell and Keith,[39] however, suggest that *bali* was from the very beginning of the nature of a tax not depending solely upon the free will of the subjects. In fact, it is hardly likely that even a kingdom of the primitive tribal type of the early Vedic age could subsist on purely voluntary contributions. In any case, in the period of the *Brāhmaṇas*, *bali* seems to have been known as a compulsory contribution payable by the subjects;[40] and, if ever voluntary it was, in the later period it may have remained so only in name. It is not unlikely that in ancient India there continued for some time the contradiction between the revenue terminology and its actual content.[41]

With the gradual development of revenue nomenclature and the emergence of new items of taxation, the word *bali* appears to be all the more intriguing in its connotation. *Bali* as used in the *Arthaśāstra* is essentially of the nature of a petty cess over and above the king's normal share of the produce,[42]

34. *CII*, iii, no. 26, l. 9; no. 27, l. 11; no. 28, l. 17 etc.
35. *Ibid.* p. 254, n. 4; p. 120, n. 1.
36. *Ibid.* no. 39, l. 68; no. 40, l. 12; no. 41, l. 14, etc.
37. *Sel. Ins.*, p. 372, n. 7; cf., *EI*, xv, pp. 293 ff; Majumdar, *History of Bengal*, i, p. 277.
38. Cf. *HRS*, pp. 4-5.
39. *Vedic Index*, ii, 62.
40. *Ait. Br.*, VII, 29.
41. R.S. Sharma, *Asbects of Political Ideas and Institutions in Ancient India*, Delhi, 1959, p. 132.
42. Ghoshal, "Some Hindu Fiscal Terms Discussed", *op. cit.*, p. 203.

whereas in the *Jātakas*[43] the term often means additional and oppressive cesses.

In contrast to the sources mentioned above, the *Milindapañho* mentions *bali* as emergency tax from which the four chief ministers are declared free.[44] This may imply that the import of the term underwent some change in post-Maurya times. But the Junagadh inscription of Rudradāman[45] (A.D. 150), which is the only epigraph of our period recording *bali* in the sense of a tax, does not corroborate the view incorporated in the *Milindapañho*. The mention of *bali* in the *Milindapañho* in the sense of an emergency levy cannot be taken to be a local variation because the area of composition of the work, and Junagadh, where the inscription of Rudradaman is found, are quite near to each other. Nor does any other source take *bali* to mean an emergency impost. It is, therefore, not unlikely that the use of *bali* in the sense of an emergency tax in the *Milindapañho* is a case of misrepresentation.

The *bali* of the inscriptions has often been taken to mean a religious tax. Thus Thomas[46] interprets the term as mentioned in the Rummindei pillar inscription of Aśoka to mean some kind of religious cess. Although the inscription of Rudradāman, where *bali* occurs in the sense of tax, records it with other fiscal terms such as *śulka* and *bhāga*, the epigraphs of the Gupta period invariably treat *bali* as one of the five sacrificial performances, the four others being *caru*, *sattra*, *vaiśvadeva* and *agnihotra*. Thus *bali* in this context cannot mean any tax. What is more important, it does not figure in the list of taxes from which the beneficiaries were generally exempted in the Gupta period and later times.

Bali is mentioned as tax mostly in legal and literary writings, which often ignore *bhāga* in its technical sense. In connection with the rate of land tax Viṣṇu[47] as well as Manu[48]

43. *Jat.* i, pp. 199, 339; ii, p. 240; iii, p. 9; v, p. 98.

44. *Milinda.*, p. 146.

45. *EI*, viii, no. 6, 14.

46. Thomas *JRAS.*, 1909 p. 467. For further discussions by Charles Lyall and K. A. Nilkanta Sastri, see *JRAS*, 1908, pp. 850-51 and *IHQ*, xx, pp. 285-287 respectively.

47. *Viṣṇu*, III. 22-23.

48. *Manu*, VII. 130.

refers to *bali* and not to *bhāga*; similar is the case with the *rājadharma* section of the *Śānti Parva*.[49] Aśvaghoṣa[50] also mentions *bali* in the sense of regular land tax. Bṛhaspati,[51] who probably belongs to the Gupta period, refers to *bali* in the same sense. At one place in the *Mahāvaṁśa*, a work of the Gupta period, the levy of *bali* is said to be very essential, which may imply that it was perhaps the basic land tax.[52] In the *Amarakośa*,[53] assignable to about the 5th century A.D., the term is used as a synonym of *śulka* and *kara* in the general sense of tax. From all this it appears that the *bali* of the Dharmasāstras and general literature is identical with the *bhāga* of the inscriptions.

Kara is another form of revenue known from our sources. As a fiscal term it appears to have been unknown to the earlier literature, but in the *Arthaśāstra* and the law-books it is of frequent occurrence. In a passage of Manu[54] it is differently interpreted by various commentators. According to Medhātithi *kara* means gifts of commodities (*dravyadānam*) and according to Sarvajñanārāyaṇa a fixed gold payment on land (*bhūminiyataṁ deyaṁ hiraṇyam*). Rāmacandra interprets the term as contribution in the form of grass, wood, etc. (*gulmadāyādikam*), and Kullūka takes it to denote contribution from villagers and townsmen either monthly or in Bhādrapada and Pauṣa (*grāmapuravāsibhyaḥ pratimāsaṁ vā bhādrapauṣa niyamena grāhyam*). According to Rāghavānanda, however, *kara* is a monthly payment by villagers (*grāmavāsibhyaḥ pratimāsikam*). The last two interpretations are very much in accordance with Bhaṭṭasvāmin's explanation of the term in his commentary on Kauṭilya.[55] Bhaṭṭasvāmin understands *kara* to mean "the annual tax paid during the months of Bhādrapada, Vasanta and the like."[56] With it may be connected the definition of *kara* in the *Arthaśāstra* text quoted by Kṣīrasvāmin,[57] i.e., it is a charge upon

49. *ŚP*, 69. 24; 72. 10.
50. *Buddhacarita*, II. 44; *Saundaranandakāvya*, II. 33.
51. *Bṛhaspati*, *āpaddharma* section, verse 20.
52. *Madhāvaṁśa*, XXVIII. 4.
53. *Amar.*, II. 8. 28.
54. *Manu*, VII. 307.
55. *AŚ*, II. 15.
56. *karaḥ prativarṣadeyaḥ bhādrapadikavasantikādyupādānam*, comm. on *AŚ*, II. 15. *JBORS*, XI, Pt. 2, pp. 83-84.
57. *pratyakaṁ sthāvarajaṅgamādideyaḥ karaḥ*, comm. on *Amar.*, II. 8, 28.

all movable and immobable articles. *Kara* thus may have been a periodical tax levied more or less universally from villagers, and it may have been realised over and above the king's normal grain-share. This is corroborated by the Junagadh inscription of Rudradāman[58] (*c.* A.D. 150), in which the king's treasury is said to have been filled by *baliśulkabhāgaiḥ* while the Sudarśana dam is said to have been built without oppressing the people with *kara*, forced labour (*viṣṭi*) and benevolences (*praṇaya*). The use of *bali* at one place and *kara* at another seems to indicate that both cannot stand for tax in general. In other words, *kara* appears to have been an oppressive impost and therefore different from, and over and above, the general land tax.

Literary, and particularly epigraphic, sources indicate that *kara* was a general tax. Aśvaghoṣa[59] takes the term in the broad sense of taxes. In the Allahabad inscription of Samudra Gupta, *kara* is used in the sense of tax in general.[60] Again, the spurious Gaya copper-plate of Samudra Gupta[61] provides that the taxpaying (*karada*) cultivators and artisans should not be allowed to settle in a certain gift village. The mention of artisans as taxpaying may indicate that *kara* is used to denote all the taxes, including those paid by the cultivators as well as the artisans. Likewise in the land grants *akaradāyī*[62] denotes one who is exempt from taxes in general. Some of the records bear expressions such as *sarvakaraparihāraih*,[63] *sarvakarasametaḥ*[64] and the like, which may simply imply that kara comprised all taxes. On the other hand, in an inscription[65] *kara* stands for all kinds of contributions other than land revenue (*bhāga*) and *bhoga*, and yet in another[66] it excludes *śulka*, *bhāga*, *bhoga*, and *hiraṇya*.

58. *EI*, viii. no. 6, ll. 15-16.
59. *Saundaranandakāvya*, II. 27.
60. *CII*, iii, no. 1, l. 22.
61. *Ibid.* no. 60, l. 13.
62. *Ibid.* no. 55, l. 26.
63. *EI*, xxiv, no. 9, l. 14.
64. *Ibid.* xxiii, no. 18, l. 10. Other expressions of a similar import used in the inscriptions are *sarvakaradānasametaḥ* (CII, iii, no. 81, l. 22), *sarvakaravisarjjitaḥ* (*Ibid.* no. 41, l. 9), *sarvakaratyāgaḥ* (*Ibid.* no. 29, l. 97). The word *kara* in these compounds bears the sense of tax in general.
65. *CII*, iii, no. 26, l. 9.
66. *EI*, i, no. 11, l. 15; vii, no. 22, l. 15.

Hence the term *kara* is used indiscriminately in both general and specific senses in varying contexts, and it is difficult to ascribe any definite meaning to it. It seems to have been some kind of land revenue, but its exact nature cannot be determined.

Like the above-mentioned items of land revenue, *hiraṇya* appears in most of the early Indian sources. The *Arthaśāstra*[67] refers to it as a branch of king's revenue. Kauṭilya[68] tells us that the *samāhartā* (collector-general) should prepare a written record (*nibandha*) specifying *inter alia* the contributions payable by the villagers severally and collectively under the heads of grain, domestic animals, *hiraṇya*, forced labour and so forth. Curiously enough, the *Arthaśāstra*[69] does not include *hiraṇya* in its regular list of constituents of the body of income (*āyaśarīram*), which suggests that in the Maurya period it was an irregular levy. The *Arthaśāstra*, however, definitely lays down a rate for its collection. In the traditional story of the origin of kingship recorded by Kauṭilya, the people, having chosen Manu as their king, undertake to contribute 1/6 of the crops, 1/10 of merchandise as well as *hiraṇya* as his share.[70] In a similar context the *Mahābhārata*[71] prescribes 1/10. Though Patañjali states that *hiraṇya* makes a king wealthy, he does not use the term in the sense of any specific land tax, let alone the question of fixing any rate of payment in this connection. But in the law-books of the post-Maurya period *hiraṇya* definitely figures as an item of king's regular revenue; and Viṣṇu[72] and Manu[73] prescribe its rate at 1/50. From the Gupta period onwards, the land grants, with the possible exception of the Vākāṭaka charters, mention this term in the list of revenues from which the donees are stated to have been exempted. But they do not give us any clue as to the rate at which *hiraṇya* was paid to the state. In any case, we can be sure that all through our period it constituted an important and established item of royal income.

67. *AŚ*, I. 13.
68. *Ibid.* II. 35.
69. *Ibid.* II. 6.
70. *AŚ*, I. 13.
71. *ŚP*, 67. 23.
72. *Viṣṇu*, III. 25.
73. *Manu*, VII. 130.

The term *hiraṇya* in the contexts referred to above, however, has been variously interpreted by different scholars. The word as occurring in the *Arthaśāstra* has been translated simply as gold.[74] The *hiraṇya* of the law-books is sometimes taken as gold, and sometimes either as a tax on the hoard or a tax on the capital of the annual income.[75] But in view of its high value, it is highly improbable that peasants paid taxes in gold.

The clue to the proper interpretation of the term, Ghoshal rightly points out,[76] is furnished by certain conditions of land revenue prevalent in later times. In the medieval period payments of the land revenue before the reform introduced by Todarmal were made in kind, but certain classes of crops (called *zabti*) were always assessed in cash on the ground that it was very difficult to divide them into shares.[77] Ghoshal, therefore, makes a reasonable guess that *hiraṇya* was a tax of this nature, more precisely, a tax in cash levied upon certain special kinds of crops as distinguished from the tax in kind which was charged upon the ordinary crops.[78] Sircar also endorses this view.[79] It may be pointed out that we have reference to a tax on certain agricultural products, collected in cash. An inscription dated A.D. 592 states that the tax for sugarcane plantation within a specified area (*vāṭa*) was 32 silver coins, though it was only 2½ silver coins if the field belonged to a religious donee.[80] It is further stated in the same record that the tax for an *allavāṭa* was half the amount prescribed above. *Alla* is the Prākṛt form of Sanskrit *ardraka*, ginger, and *allavāṭa* may possibly mean 'a ginger plantation.' Since taxes on certain types of products were paid in cash, we may expect that *hiraṇya* was levied on commercial crops.

Although several Kauṭilyan items of land revenue continued down to the Gupta period, the case is different with irrigation tax (*udakabhāga*), an important revenue head of the

74. Shamasastry, *Arthaśāstra* (Tr.), seventh edition, p. 158.
75. N.C. Bandopadhyaya, *Kauṭilya*, pp. 139, 140.
76. *HRS*, p. 61.
77. For reference see *ibid.* p. 62.
78. *Ibid.* p. 62.
79. *Sel. Ins.*, p. 372.
80. *EI*, xxx, no. 30, l. 20.

Maurya state,[81] which constructed reservoirs filled with water, either perennial or drawn from other sources.[82] This tax is mentioned by Kauṭilya in the chapter on the cultivation of crown lands under the supervision of the superintendent of agriculture (*sītādhyakṣa*),[83] and therefore Ghoshal takes it to refer to royal farms.[84] But a closer examination of the *Arthaśāstra* material suggests that the *uḍakabhāga* refers to non-crown lands. It is stated in the *Arthaśāstra* that the crown tenants should receive ½ of the yield when they employ their own capital and 1/4 or 1/5 when the state supplies the implements and other necessaries.[85] In the first case the state would receive ½ and in the second it would get 3/4 or 4/5. If in addition to this, the state received a water tax at the rate of 1/5, 1/4 and 1/3 as the case was, then practically nothing would be left to the crown tenants. Thus it appears probable that water taxes were levied from the cultivators of non-crown lands. But it is not known whether in the Mauryan period the irrigation levy was collected from the peasants in addition to the land tax or the latter was inclusive of the former.

There is a conspicuous lack of consolidated evidence in regard to irrigation in post-Maurya and Gupta times; and the scattered references that we get do not point to anything like irrigation levy (*udakabhāga*) of Maurya times.[86] Nor does it figure in the long list of taxes from which brāhmaṇas or beneficiaries were exempted in post-Maurya and Gupta land grants.[87]

The absence of irrigation tax in our period might have been at least in part due to the fact that the state generally ceased to bear the main responsibility for irrigation and consequently could not claim any cess for that reason.[88] Manu's injunction against the seizure of houses, tanks, orchards, and fields by others may mean that tanks were owned and construct-

81. *AŚ*, II. 24.
82. *Ibid.* II. 1.
83. *Ibid.* II. 24.
84. *HRS*, p. 31.
85. *AŚ*, II. 24.
86. *Ibid.* II. 24.
87. R. S. Sharma, *Light on Early Indian Society and Economy*, Bombay, 1966, p. 100.
88. *Ibid.*

ed by individuals for irrigational purposes.[89] Manu ordains that amongst other things selling one's own tank, garden, wife or child is a sin to be expiated by penance.[90] Again, Nārada states that if a man were to repair a dike without the permission of its owner, he shall not be entitled to profit out of it.[91] Thus the law-books seem to suggest some kind of individual management of irrigation tanks, dams, reservoirs, etc., which, in turn, means that irrigation might have been to a certain extent an individual concern. Dion Chrysostom (c. A.D. 50-117) also informs us that in order to convey water from large and small rivers in India, the local inhabitants made many channels.[92]

That the individual initiative and cooperative efforts played considerable part is borne out by a number of inscriptions from the Śaka-Kuṣāṇa and Gupta periods and is also supported by the law-books of the early centuries of the Christian era.[93] However, the state did not entirely cease to bear responsibility for irrigation. The Hathigumpha inscription[94] of Khāravela, the Junagadh inscriptions of Rudradāman[95] and Skanda Gupta[96] among others testify to the royal initiative in this sphere. Probably the state spent its resources only on the implementation of comparatively bigger projects, beyond the means of an individual. Thus with limited state initiative in the sphere of irrigation in post-Maurya and Gupta times, there remained perhaps no justification for any regular irrigation levy (*udakabhāga*) of the Maurya period.

The disappearance of the Mauryan *udakabhāga* in the post-Maurya and Gupta times need not necessarily mean a fall in the burden of taxation. For unlike the terms discussed above, we come across certain fiscal expressions such as *uparikara* and *udraṅga*, which are mentioned in inscriptions only from

89. *Manu*, VIII. 264.
90. *Ibid.* XI. 62.
91. *Nārada*, XI. 20. cf. *Yāj.*, II. 157.
92. Oratio, XXXV, 434, McCrindle, *Ancient India as described in Classical Literature*, p. 175.
93. R. S. Sharma, *Light on Early Indian Society and Economy*, pp. 100-101.
94. *EI*, xx, no. 7, l. 3.
95. *Ibid.* viii, no. 6, ll. 9-16.
96. *CII*, iii, no. 14, l. 17.

the Gupta period[97] onwards and do not occur in any pre-Gupta source. According to Fleet[98] the word *uparikara* is derived from *upari* or *upri* and means "a tax levied from the cultivators who had no proprietory rights in the soil." In inscriptions, however, the word is recorded invariably with *udraṅga*, which has led Ghoshal to suggest that the two fiscal terms are used antithetically. He thus explains *udraṅga* as a tax levied from the permanent tenants and *uparikara* as a tax imposed on the temporary ones.[99] He associates *uparikara* with the Marathi word *upri*, which means a cultivator not belonging originally to a village, but residing and occupying land in it, either upon a lease for a stipulated term of years, or at the pleasure of the proprietory. The evidence for this, it has been suggested, is very tenuous, since the Marathi language developed ten centuries after the date of our inscriptions.[100] The same is true of Fleet's interpretation. Moreover, in most land grants the two terms occur together, and if *uparikara* and *udraṅga* mean taxes on temporary and permanent tenants respectively, it would imply that a certain piece of donated land was cultivated both by permanent and temporary tenants simultaneously which obviously seems absurd. Of course, in case of village grants[101] the presence of both types of tenants cannot be altogether discounted, but in the case of charters which record the grant of pieces of land[102] with the assignment of *uparikara* and *udraṅga* this could not have been possible. Nor is there any independent evidence to show that the government used to impose any extra special tax on temporary and permanent tenants. There is besides no reason why the state records should distinguish the tax paid by the permanent tenants from that obtained from the temporary ones.[103]

97. *CII*, iii, no. 21. l. 12; no. 22, l. 16; no. 23; l. 7; no. 26, l.8; no. 29, l. 9, no. 31, l. 8; no 38, l. 26; *EI*, viii, no. 28, l. 17. Senart thinks that *sakarukara* of a Sātavāhana grant (*EI*, vii, no. 7 (14), 1.3) is the natural equivalent of *sodraṅga soparikara*. This view, as Senart himself recognises, is wholly conjectural, although there is nothing improbable in the *udraṅga* and *uparikara* taxes going back to the Sātavahana period. (*HRS*, pp. 188-189).

98. *CII*, iii, p. 98, n. l.

99. *HRS*, p. 210.

100. Maity, *op. cit.*, p. 61.

101. *CII*, iii, nos. 21, 22, 23, 26 etc.

102. *Ibid.* no. 38.

103. Altekar, *Raṣtrakutas and their Times*, Poona, 1934, p. 216.

Barnett rejects the view of Ghoshal altogether, and suggests that *uparikara* is something like the Tamil *melvaram*, i.e., crown's share of the produce. According to Alaekar,[104] on the other hand, *uparikara* is identical with *bhoga* which consisted of contributions in the shape of articles of provisions. Both the contentions, however, appear erroneous in the context of the Gupta evidence. In the Karitalai copper-plate inscriptiod of the Mahārāja Jayanātha dated A.D. 493-94[105] the terms *uparikara* and *udraṅga* occur, as also the expression *bhāgabhogakara*. Therefore *uparikara* can neither be equated with *bhāga*, the crown's share of produce which is indicated by *melvaram* in Tamil, nor with *bhoga*. Since *upari* in Sanskrit, Hindi and Bengali means 'upon' or 'extra',[106] it perhaps has led Sircar[107] to explain *uparikara* as an 'extra cess'. But it must be admitted that none of the explanations so far offered is conclusive. The interpretation of the term bristles with difficulty, particularly because of the conspicuous reticence of the literary sources on the subject.

It is equally difficult to interpret the term *udraṅga*, which like *uparikara* occurs only in the land grants and not in the literature of the period. Bühler,[108] first of all, pointed out that the *Sāsvatakoṣa* gives for *udraṅga* the equivalents *uddhāra* and *udgrantha*. Following this source, Fleet takes *udraṅga* to mean the share of the produce usually collected for the king.[109] But we have already noted that sometimes *udraṅga* and *bhāga*, which probably means the regular land tax, occur in one and the same grant, and therefore it is not likely that the former could mean king's own usual grain-share. Ghoshal,[110] on the other hand, interprets *udraṅga* as a tax on permanent tenants and has been supported by Sircar[111] in this contention. But the explanation is untenable for the reasons given above. Maity offers two alternative explanations. According to the

104. *Ibid.* p. 216.
105. *CII*, iii, no. 26, ll. 8-9.
106. Maity, *op. cit.*, p. 62.
107. *Sel. Ins.*, p. 2666 n.
108. *IA*, xii, p. 189, n. 39.
109. *CII*, iii, pp. 97-98. Altekar is also of the view that *udraṅga* meant *bhaga*, the normal land tax (Altekar, *op. cit.*, p. 216).
110. Ghoshal, *op. cit.*, p. 210.
111. *Sel. Ins.*, p. 371, n. 5.

first, *udraṅga* may have been an anomalous derivative of the Sanskrit word *udaka* and thus may have meant something like a water tax.[112] But, as has been shown above, we have no independent evidence to prove the prevalence of anything like water-tax in the Gupta period. According to another explanation given by Maity,[113] *udraṅga* may be the same thing as *draṅga* which according to the *Rājataraṅgiṇī*,[114] a late work, is a watch-station; and the term may have stood for a police tax levied on the district for the maintenance of the local police station. This view is more or less endorsed by Puspa Niyogi.[115] It is difficult to say anything with certitude either in favour or against the plausibility of this explanation. Probably, like *uparikara*, *udraṅga* may have also been a levy over and above the usual grain share, though any attempt to determine its exact nature will only be conjectural unless some fresh evidence is forthcoming.

The land grants of the Gupta period mention several other terms such as *halikākara*,[116] *ditya*,[117] *meya*,[118] or *tulyameya*[119] and *dhānya*[120], none of which is referred to in any source other than the contemporary epigraphs. No indication is available in earlier or contemporary sources about the meaning of *halikākara*, which is recorded only in two land charters of the Ucchakalpa ruler Sarvanātha,[121] who seems to have ruled in the Baghelkhand region in the last part of the fifth century and the early part of the sixth. Ghoshal suggests that *halikākara* may mean a tax on ploughs.[122] What, however, may have been the precise nature of a tax on ploughs is not possible to ascertain. Maity opines that the above-mentioned term may

112. Maity, *op. cit.*, p. 62.
113. *Ibid.*
114. *Rājataraṅginī* (Stein's trans.), ii, pp. 291-92.
115 *Contribution to the Economic History of Northern India*, Calcutta, 1962, p. 187
116 *EI*, xix, no 21, l 10; *CI*, iii, no 30, l. 13
117 *EI*, x, no 13, l. 6; xi, no 21, l. 11
118 *CII*, iii, no. 60, l. 12; EI, ii, no. 30, l. 8; iv, no. 16, l. 9., ix, no. 53, l. 9; x, no. 16, l. 15.
119. *EI*, vii, no. 22, l. 15.
120. *Ibid.* xxxi, no. 35, l. 12; no. 39, l. 21; *CII*, iii, no. 38, l. 26.
121. The Sohawal copper-plates of the year 191, *EI*, xix, no. 21, l. 10; the Khoh copper-plates of the year 197, *CII*, iii, no. 30, l. 13.
122. *HRS*, p. 213.

connote an extra tax imposed upon the area which could be cultivated by one plough.[123] Although *bali* as a measure of land does seem to be the likely object of a special tax, there is evidence to imply that in later times land was sometimes taxed according to its area.[124] On the other hand, we know that plough taxes were levied from the people down to Mughal times.[125] Even though taxes on ploughs and on the area of cultivation may have been in vogue in later times, this cannot be taken to suggest conclusively that *halikakara* stood for either. The exact meaning of the term, therefore, appears to be uncertain.

The word *ditya*, which occurs in the Surat plates of the Traikuṭaka king Vyāghrasena, literally means "that which is to be given."[126] The expression is recorded in the inscriptions as *sarvadityaviṣṭiparihāreṇa* meaning exemption from all dues and forced labour. This may mean that *ditya* denoted all taxes except forced labour and thus appears to have a very wide connotation.

The term *meya*, which is mentioned in some eastern as well as central Indian epigraphs of the Gupta period, is generally followed by the term *hiraṇya*. In the Madhuban copper-plate inscription of Harṣa,[127] however, the term is recorded as *yathāsamucitatulyameyabhāgabhogakara*. *Tulyameya* here may have been used as an adjective of *bhāgabhogakara*, and the entire expression may thus mean the king's normal revenue in kind that can be weighed and measured. But in the Gupta records *meya* does not occur along with *bhāgabhogakara*, which makes it likely that *meya* was a substitute for a general land tax known as *bhāga*.

The term *dhānya* also appears to have denoted the general land tax. Most land grants mention *dhānyabhogakara* in place of *bhāgabhogakara*, which shows that *dhānya* occurs in place of *bhāga*. The Kurud plates of Narendra of the year 24, palaeographically assignable to the 5th century A.D., however,

123. Maity, *op. cit.*, p. 63.

124. *Cambridge History of India*, iv, p. 450.

125. *Ibid.* p. 454.

126. *EI*, ix, no. 21, l. 11.

127. *Ibid.* vii, no. 22, l. 15.

records *dhārya* with *bhoga* and *bhāga.*[128] Again, a grant of the Maitraka ruler Dharmasena II bears the expression *sad-hānyabhāgabhogahiraṇyadeya.*[129] This may be taken to imply a distinction between *bhāga bhoga* on the one hand and *dhānya* on the other. Ghoshal suggests that probably *dhānya* was a fixed contribution in kind and *bhāga* a share of the produce.[130] The expressions *dhānya*, *meya* and *ditya*, however do not appear together in our inscriptions, which may imply that all the three carry more or less the same connotation, though *ditya* may have had a comparatively wider application.

It would appear from the foregoing discussion that several fiscal terms indicating taxes on land in the *Arthaśāstra* continued to be in use down to the Gupta period, though their precise meaning in the context of changing times may not be clearly understood. Thus such taxes as *bhāga*, *kara* and *hiraṇya* of the *Arthaśāstra* find mention not only in the *Smṛtis* but also in the land grants of the later period. On the other hand, *piṇḍakara* and *udakabhāga* do not occur in the later sources, which may to a certain extent preclude the possibility of their existence in the Gupta period.

Certain new land revenue terms such as *uparikara*, *udraṅga* and *halikākara* appear for the first time in the Gupta period. In addition to these there may have been several other taxes in existence at that time, because the enumeration of taxes in the contemporary inscriptions is usually followed by the word *ādi* or *ityādi* (etcetra). We may add that in a few Pallava charters donees are granted land with eighteen *parihāras*, though all of them are not enumerated.[131] The Basim grant of the Vākāṭaka king Vindhyaśakti II records as many as fourteen *parihāras.*[132] While all these may point to an increased burden of taxation in the Gupta period, the incidence of all the taxes may not have fallen on every individual tax-payer.

128. *Ibid.* xxi, no. 35, l. 12.
129. *IA*, vii, p. 72.
130. *HRS*, p. 219.
131. *Sel. Ins.*, pp. 439-40; *EI*, xv, no. 11, ll.
132. *Sel. Ins.*, pp. 408-9.

II

LAND REVENUE IN EARLY MEDIEVAL NORTH INDIA (c. 600—1200 A.D.)

B. P. Mazumdar

Early medieval literature and inscriptions indicate, though not fully explain, the sources of revenues from land and its products. Inscriptions do not enumerate all taxes but refer to many unnamed taxes which could be collected by the recipients of grants of lands by kings and feudatories. The words used for such taxes are *akiñcit pragrāhyāḥ* in Pāla and Sena inscriptions, *ādibhiḥ* in Somavaṁśī inscriptions, *niyatāniyata samastādāyān* in Gāhaḍavāla charters, *sarvādāyasametaḥ* in Paramāra, *ucitānucitam* or *aparairapi* in Candella and *samastarājapratyādāya* in Kalacuri records.

All types of land, excepting the *bhūmichidra* lands, were taxable. The Kamauli plate of Vaidyadeva states that *bhūchidrañcha akiñcitkaragrāhyam*, uncultivable or uncultivated land given in grant, is not taxable.[1] The Arabs of Sindh levied taxes on both irrigated and unirrigated lands. The commentators of the *Smṛtis* recommend different rates of taxes according to the fertility of land or labour involved in the production of a crop.

The compound word *bhāgabhogakara* is more frequently mentioned than any other tax in early medieval inscriptions. Excepting the Pañcāla group,[2] all the land-grants of the Gāhaḍavāla kings mention *bhāgabhogakara*. *Bhāgabhoga* occurs in the inscriptions of the Pālas, the Gurjara-Pratihāras, the Paramāras, the Caulukyas, the Kalacuris, the Candellas, the Somavaṁśīs, and in the records of the feudatories of the Gāhaḍavālas in Shahabad. It may be mentioned here that *bhāga-*

1. *EI*, xix, p. 121 f.n. 3.

2. According to Roma Niyogi the two Chandrāvatı inscriptions of Chandradeva, Basahi and Kamauli grants of Mahārājaputra Govindacandra and the Sarnath inscription of Kumāradevī, which belong to the pañcāla group, refer to such taxes as *bhāga*, *bhāgabhāga* (*bhoga* ?), *bhogabhāga*.

bhoga taxes were not allowed to be collected by the donees who received lands in the kingdoms of the Rāṣṭrakūṭas, the Cāhamānas, Senas and the Eastern Ganga kings of Orissa. The term *rājakīyabhoga* occurs in the Sanderav inscription of the Naḍḍula Cāhamāna king Kelhaṇa.[3] *Rājabhogakara* occurs in the Barrackpur plate of Vijayasena and the Naihati plate of Vallālasena[4] and not in any inscription of his successors. *Chāgakara* is mentioned in the Jabalpur plates of the Kalacuri king Jayasiṁha, dated A.D. 1167[5].

Altekar and following him Roma Niyogi have wrongly suggested that *bhāga* and *bhoga* were the alternative forms of *udraṅga* and *uparikara* respectively,[6] because they take the place of *udraṅga* and *uparikara* in many inscriptions. But the non-mention of particular items of taxes in an inscription does not mean that they were not collected from the subjects. Thus *rājabhogakara* occurs in the land grants of Vijayasena and Vallālasena but not in those of Lakṣmaṇasena and his successors. This does not necessarily imply that *rājabhoga* ceased to be levied since the reign of Lakṣmaṇasena ; on the other hand the privilege of collecting *rājabhoga* may not have been conceded to the donees who received lands from Lakṣmaṇasena and his successors. Secondly, there are instances of the mention of both *uparikara* and *bhoga* in one copper-plate. Dasaratha Sharma and Asoka Majumdar point out that both the taxes occur in the Nausari plates of the Caulukya king Karṇa. We may produce other instances from the Nalanda plates of Dharmapāla, Bhagalpur plates of Nārāyaṇapāla and the Mandhata plates of Vākpati Amoghavarṣa and Jayasiṁha of the Paramāra dynasty.[7]

It seems that among the words *bhāga*, *bhoga*, *kara*, *udraṅga*, *uparikara*, etc., *bhāga* connotes land revenue. *Kara* ceased to mean any specific tax in early medieval north India, and the term is not used in the Gāhaḍavāla and Candella

3. *EI*, xi, p. 47.
4. *IB*, iii, pp. 67, 79.
5. *CI*, iv. p. 329.
6. Altekar : *Rastrakuṭas and their Times*, p. 214;
Niyogi, *History of the Gāhaḍavāla Dynasty*, Calcutta, 1959. p. 168.
7. *IA*, vi, p. 53, line 20 *sahiraṇyabhāgabhogaḥ soparikara* in Vākpati's inscription *EI*, iii, p. 49, *sahiraṇya bhāgabhogaḥ soparikara* in Jayasiṁha's inscription.

inscriptions in this sense. Our doubts about the nature of *kara* as a tax is further confirmed in the Monghyr copper-plate of Devapāla. In this inscription the word *kara* is not enumerated along with different and specific items of taxes but mentioned along with unnamed taxes *samucit karahiraṇyādisarvapratyāopanaḥ kārya iti*. Further, neither *udraṅga* nor *uparikara* is mentioned in any *nibandha* or digest of early medieval period of Indian history. *Bhoga*, if we are to rely on digests and commentaries, as the one written by Abhyatilaka Gani, meant periodical supplies.

An attempt may be made to determine the specific rate of land revenue as covered by the term *bhāga*. Bṛhaspati, like Gautama, prescribes that the lowest rate of land revenue (*bhāga*) is one-tenth—a rate which is higher than that recommended by Manu VII. 130[8]. Both Bṛhaspati and the *Viṣṇudharmottara* ordain that the varying rates of grain-share of the king shall depend on the nature of crops grown in different seasons. So, cultivators shall pay to the king one-tenth, the lowest rate, if the produce is derived from fallow lands, one-eighth on crops grown in rainy season and one-sixth on those grown in spring season.[9] The commentators of Manu, such as Medhātithi, Kullūkabhaṭṭa and Mitra Miśra, also agree that the rate of land revenue varies according to the nature and fertility of the soil. Medhātithi, Govindarāja and Kullūkabhaṭṭa do not differ from the opinion of Manu, who prescribes that husbandmen shall give 1/8th of grain in normal times and 1/4th in emergency.[10] Lakṣmīdhara also quotes with approval the views of Manu and holds that 1/4th shall be collected even from the kṣatriyas during emergency.[11] Mitra Miśra, explaining one of the verses of the *Bṛhaspatismṛti*, states that cultivators shall pay from the corns produced in fallow lands (*khila*) one-tenth, from corns grown in rainy season one-eighth and those grown in the spring season one-sixth. In the spring, he adds, is cultivated *śukadhānya* like wheat and barley. In short, if we are to rely on the views

8. Manu says that the royal share of the produce is 1/6, 1/8 and 1/12.

9. *Rājanītiprakāśa*, Chowkhamba Sanskrit Series, pp. 262-263.

10. *Manusmṛti* X. 118 and 120. Kullūka on Manu X. 118 comments *rājño dhānyā linānamaṣtamu ityādḥyuktaṁ sa āpadi dhānyādeścaturthamapi.*

11. *Rājadharmakāṇḍa*, (GOS. No. C), p. 89.

of Bṛhaspati, the *Viṣṇudharmottara* and Mitra Miśra the highest rate of land revenue was one-sixth, which was collected from the growers of such spring crops as wheat and barley. For the crops sown during the rains, namely rice, the rate was one-eighth. The *Viṣṇudharmottara*, as quoted in the *Rājanītiprakāśa*, and the *Agni Purāṇa* also inform us that one-sixth of wheat or barley and one-eighth of śimvīdhānya, that is, crops grown in pods, shall be taken by the king.

Inscriptions do not give any idea about fixation of the rate of land revenue; they only suggest that rates varied according to the types of land. The Damodarpur copper-plate of Gupta times show that fallow or *khila* lands were assessed at a lower rate than the average type of cultivable lands. An undated document preserved in the *Lekhapaddhati* shows that whereas one had to pay for *uddhakhilabhūmi* 16 *drammas* per *vimśopaka*, and for *khilabhumi* 10 *drammas* per *vimśopaka*. The Mehar plates of Dāmodaradeva (A.D. 1234) shows that those lands which were never brought under cultivation (*cirakhila*) were not assessed. These plates also show that *nālabhūmi* or cultivable land was assessed at a lower rate than homestead or *vāstu lands*.

Early medieval inscriptions of northern India refer to taxes on a number of agricultural products. Inscriptions of Jayabhaṭa III and IV of the early Gurjara and Allaśakti of the Sendraka dynasties speak of the right of collection of *dhānya*, apparently a tax on paddy, from the people.[12] The Rāṣṭrakūṭa king Govinda IV allowed the brāhmaṇa donees inhabiting the western boundary of Manyakheta in A.D. 930 to collect *hiraṇya* and *dhānya* as taxes.[13] Altekar informs us that the Gangas and Bāṇas, who sometimes became feudatories of the Raṣṭrakūṭas, levied taxes on paddy.[14] Kalhaṇa and medieval digests, including the one written by Vardhmāna of Mithilā, refer to collection of shares of śasya or corn by the king.

Like paddy, wheat and barley were also taxed. The Paramāra Jaitrasiṁha levied a cess of one *seī* of Koraḍa corn

12. *CII*, iv. pp. 86, 89, 95, 109 for Early Gurjaras and p. 122 for Sendrakas.

13. *EI*, xxiii. p. 107.

14. *Op. cit.*, pp. 218-19.

on an area cultivated by one plough in the Mangalana area in A. D. 1217.[15] Vikramasiṁha, the Kacchapaghāṭa king, assigned a tax of one *viṁśopaka* coin charged on each *goṇi* of wheat in the neighbhourhood of Gwalior.[16] Specific references to the levy of tax on wheat and barley corns are found in inscriptions of the Rajputana, Gwalior and Malwa regions. The Cāhamāna king Aśvarāja assigned the income of one *hāraka* of barley corn from four villages, where wells with water-wheels were utilised for irrigation, for the temple of Semipati.[17] The Arthuna inscription of Cāmuṇḍarāja (A.D. 1080) refers not only to the assignment of one *hāraka* of barley but several other important agricultural products like cotton and candied sugar to the donee. The Candella and Paramāra kings gathered some portion of sugarcane as revenue.[18] It is surprising that the inscriptions of the Uttar Pradesh, Bihar and Bengal do not make any reference to the right of levies on sugarcane to the donees., nor do they refer to levy of cass on cotton-producing trees (*karpāśa*).

Not only rice, wheat and barley, but also the stalks of these plants, used as fodder, were taxed. Sometimes taxes associated with these products did not end there. The Rajor inscriptions of Mathanadeva, dated A.D. 960, the Karitalai inscription of Lakṣmaṇarāja II and Bargaon stone-inscription of Śabara refer to *khalabhikṣā*, which has been explained by Kielhorn and Ghoshal as 'beggings from the threshing floor'.[19] Puspa Niyogi suggests that the term denotes 'an additional collection in kind from the grain brought to the threshing floor.'[20]

The Dharmaśāstras recommend that the king shall levy taxes on trees, perfumes, medicinal herbs, flowers, roots, fruits, leaves, vegetables and grass. All these sources of revenue

15. *IA*, xii, p. 85. The editor of the Mangalana inscription tells us that in Marwar, *Mung*, *motha*, *chanā* and *gavāra* are collectively called *koraḍa*.

16. *EI*, ii, p. 232.

17. Sevadi Inscription *EI*, xi. pp. 28f.

18. *EI*, xx, p. 130 (Charkhari plat of Paramārdideva, A.D. 1178; *IA*, xvi, p. 208 (Augasi plate of Devavardan, A.D. 1134.

19. *EI*, iii. p. 264 f.n. ; Ghoshal, *HRS*, p. 237.

20. P. Niyogi, *Contribution to the Economic History of Northern India*, p. 184.

were also tapped in early medieval India. Lakṣmīdhara quotes with approval the views of Manu.[21] Sarvajñanārāyaṇa explains the word *prītibhogam* in Manu VIII. 307 as *phalakukummaśākhātṛṇādyspāyaṁ pratidināgrāhyam* of daily presents in the form of fruits, flowers, vegetables, grass etc. Asoka Majumdar thinks that the expression *vrikṣamālakulakāṣṭhotṛṇodakopetaḥ* in many Caulukya inscriptions should not mean that they belonged to the king but "this recital was necessary to make the gift valid."[22] It is difficult to accept this view, because in many Caulukya inscriptions the above-mentioned expression does not occur. For example, the donee of a grant of Ajayapāla in A.D. 1175 received the right to levy taxes on *vṛksamālā kulaśvatuḥ kaṇṭakaviśuddhaḥ.*[23] In inscription of dynasties other than those of the Caulukyas of Gujarat, the formula mentioned by Asoka Majumdar for making a grant of land valid, do not occur. Thus though trees, fruits and flowers were taxable, the right of taxation on these items was not always given to the donees. Let us take an example from the inscriptions of the Candellas. While in A.D. 988 Dhaṅga transferred the right over *āmaramadhukaṁ* to the donee, Devavarman in A.D. 1050 gifted away *āmaramadhukaḥ svasaivālaḥ svasimātṛnayuti*, Madanavarman in A.D. 1134 and Paramārdi in A.D. 1178 allowed the donees the right to levy cess on a large number of items including *śaṇekṣukarpāśa kusuma śaṇāmramadhukādi.*[24]

Fruits were another source of revenue. Mangoes were enjoyed by the beneficiaries who received land grants from kings of Bengal and Bihar, Orissa, Uttar Pradesh, Madhya Pradesh, etc. Similarly, *madhuka* figures as a source of revenue practically all over northern India. Coconuts occur in Sena and Paramāra inscriptions and also in grants from Orissa as items of taxes given over to the donees. Betelnuts (*pūga*) are mentioned n Kalacuri, Varman, Caulukya and Sena inscriptions. But betel leaves as sources of revenue are mentioned only in some Sena inscriptions and the *Likhanāvalī* of Vidyāpati.

21. *Rājadharmakāṇda*, pp. 88-89.

22. *Caulukyas of Gujarat*, Bombay, 1956, p. 248.

23. *IA*, xviii, p. 83.

24. *Ibid.* xvi, pp. 203-208 (for Dhaṅga and Devavarman); *EI*, xx. p. 130 (for Paramārdi).

A few other fruits also brought income to the state. Grapes were a source of income to the Arab rulers of Sindh. The Belava copper-plate of Bhojavarman is the only inscription in Bengal which refers to jack-fruit (*panasa*) as a taxable fruit.[25] Black pepper (*marica*) and dried ginger (*śuṇṭhī*) are mentioned only in inscriptions of Yuvarāja II Kalacuri.[26] Madder and *solonum melongana* are mentioned as sources of income in inscriptions of Gujarat[27] and Banswara in Rajputana.[28]

Pasture lands continued to be sources of revenue in early medieval India. *Gocara* as a tax is mentioned in the Kadi grant of Mūlarāja and numerous Gāhaḍavāla, Paramāra and Candella land grants. The *Lekhapaddhati* and the commentary to Dvyāśraya (III. verse 18) by Abhayatilaka Gaṇi inform us that in Gujarat, villagers had to pay an annual tax on grazing lands. The *Lekhapaddhati* also gives the following additional details :

Tax for grazing fields for cows and buffaloes	2 *drammas*
,, ,, ,, ,, ,, oxen..	1 *dramma*
,, ,, ,, ,, ,, rams, sheep....	½ *dramma*

But for bullocks, engaged in ploughing fields, the owner of the bullocks had not to pay such a tax if they grazed on these grounds.

Mode of assessment

Assessment of revenue was obviously based on the measurement of land. The following measurements continued in the post-Gupta period : *aṅgula*, *hasta*, *dhanu*, *daṇḍa*, *nala*, *nivartana*, *kulyavāpa*, *pādāvarta*, *droṇavāpa*, *āḍhavāpa*, *pāṭaka*, and *khaṇḍa*. But in early medieval India some new *hasta* measures were introduced. In the Sena kingdom there obtained such measures as *samataṭīyanala*, *vṛsabhaśankaranala*, standards of 22 and 32 cubits in the reign of Lakṣmaṇasena. The *hasta* measure current in the then Gwalior area was

25. *IB*, iii. p. 21, l. 38.
26. *CII*, iv. pp. 215, 223.
27. *IA*, xli, p. 20.
28. *EI*, xiv. p. 300 ff.

known as *parameśvarīyahasta*.[29] The *hala*, *bhūmi*, *pāśa*, *nāluka*, *vaha*, *sira* measures are new methods of measuring lands. The use of *pāśa* measure during the reign of Bhīma II Caulukya[30] shows that long before the Mughal period chains, possibly made of iron, were used for measuring lands in northern India.

Revenues were assessed on an individual and not on a collective basis. We do not come across a single inscription of our period which shows that villagers paid taxes collectively. Further, excepting Gujarat, there was possibly no arrangement for fixation of revenues permanently on a land.[31] The Anjaneri plates of Bhogaśakti refer to fixed taxes, but those were the privileges granted to merchants. As we know from the *Dvyaśraya* and the *Lekhapaddhati*, payment was made directly by the peasants as well as through intermediaries.

Mode of payment

People had the option of paying in both cash and kind. Merutuṅga, while referring to the failure of cultivators in paying revenues to Bhīma I Caulukya, tells us of such dues as the *rājadeyavibhāga* and *śasyanidānibhūta dānī samvandhe*,[32] that is, dues payable to the king and the royal share that was to be deducted from the grain produced. The documents, excepting one, recorded in the *Lekhapaddhati* show payment of revenue in kind. Asoka Majumdar concludes that as years rolled on the people of Gujarat pre ferred to pay the taxes in cash. In Kashmir, as the *Rājataraṅgiṇī* and the *Lokaprakaśa* tell us, a greater portion of land revenue was collected in *khāris* of grain.[33] Kalhaṇa gives specific reference to rice being paid as land revenue in the reign of Sussala (A.D. 1112-1120). In eastern India, both modes of payment, cash and kind, were prevalent. The Khalimpur copper-plate of Dharmapāla refers to one *ṣaṣṭhādhikṛta* and *bhogapati* as officials who were informed of the land grant. *Bhoga*, if the *Lekhapaddhati* is to be relied upon, was some pay-

29. Vaillabhaṭṭasvāmin temple inscription, *EI*. i, pp. 154 ff.
30. *IA*, xviii. pp. 110 ff.
31. *Chaulukyas of Gujarat*, p. 244.
32. *Prabandhacintāmaṇi*, ed. Jinavijaya Muni, p. 53.
33. *Rājataraṅgiṇī*, ed. Stein, ii, pp. 328 ff.

ment in kind. That book contains a letter mentioning forty *kalasīs* and four *muṭakas* of peas as *bhoga.*[34] However, the Silimpur stone-inscription, whose characters belong to the eleventh century, records that, prahāsa refused to accept 900 gold coins and the gift of landed property yielding an income of 1000 coins from Jayapāla, who may have been a Pāla king of Kāmarūpa.[35] In the Barrackpur copper-plate of Vijayasena,[36] Naihati plate of Vallālasena, Anulia, Govindapur, Tarpandighi plates of Lakṣmaṇasena, Madanpāḍā and Sāhitya Parisat plates of Viśvarūpasena, we find references to the incomes mostly in cash from different types of lands in the Puṇḍravardhana *bhukti*, south Rāḍha or Burdwan division. The Mehar plate of Dāmodaradeva, dated A.D. 1234, also refers to the annual revenue (*sāmvatsarika hiraṇya*) from different types of land like fallow, cultivable, homestead, mixed and lands with mounds.[37] In Orissa we have several references to the annual land revenues payable to the king in inscriptions of the Gaṅgas of Kaliṅganagarā. In one instance it was five silver coins (*rūpañchadeḍhaḥ*) to be paid in the month of Phālguna every year.[38] In two other cases they are two *māḍa* or gold coins annually[39] and four *palas* of silver.[40] The inscriptions of Mahābhavagupta Janamejaya I of the Somavaṁśi dynasty and of Gayaḍatuṅga also refer to annual revenues of five and four *palas* of silver.[41] Thus, in eastern India the tendency of paying land revenue in cash was increasingly becoming popular. Though *rājabhoga* in the sense of payment in kind is mentioned in the Barrackpore and Naihati plates of Vijayasena and Vallālasena respectively, yet it does

34. *Lekhapaddhati*, p. 9.

35. *EI*, xiii, pp. 283 ff.

36. *pāṭakacatuṣṭaya kaparddakapurāṇaśatadvayotpattiḥ.* Though *utpatti* literally means income, here we should translate it as revenue, because, income from land cannot be stationary. It is just like the fixation of rates by the municipality.

37. I have accepted the readings and interpretation of Dr. D. C. Sircar and not of Dr. N. P. Chakravarti, both of whom edited the plate in the *EI*.

38. *EI*, xxxi, 317 ff (Chipurupalli pls. of Vajrahasta Anantavarman).

39. Rajaguru, S. N. : *Inscription of Orissa*, ii, p. 224.

40. *EI*, IV, pp. 198-201.

41. Cf., *EI*, xxviii, p. 47; JPASB, i, pp. 12-13.

not figure in any of the grants of their successors. So it seems probable that payment of land revenue in cash became the rule in the post-Vallāla Bengal.

Concluding remarks

A perusal of the eulogistic inscriptions and books written during the period under survey conveys an impression that early medieval kings did not levy heavy taxes. The Kavi and Prince of Wales Museum plates of the early Gurjara king Jayabhaṭa IV tell us that "these people (subjects of Jayabhaṭa IV) are made to fold their hands and to bow to him, who resembles the disc of the cresccent moon (since he is possessed of brilliance) has an increasing splendour of the body, and levies light taxes (even as the moon looks lovely, increases in size and sheds tender rays)."[42] Huan Tsang also informs us that during the reign of Harṣavardhana "taxation being light, and forced service being sparingly used, every one keeps to his hereditary occupation and attends to his patrimony."[43] But Arab Muslim travellers like al Idrisi record that the subjects of the Rāṣṭrakūṭa kingdom paid heavy taxes and consequently the king was immensely rich.[44] The *Lekhapaddhati* preserves a letter, which mentions a word *chaṭāpaka* which means an increase in revenue.[45] This suggests people were made to pay more taxes for agricultural products and more land revenue in Gujarat. This was also true of the other parts of India. Caṇḍeśvara, the fourteenth century Maithila statesman-scholar, explains away the term *ṣaḍbhāga* as a figurative term. He recommends that so long as subjects do not feel the burden of taxation too heavy to bear, the king may levy such increasing taxes as to meet the expenses and other necessities of the government.[46] A study of the *Rājataraṅgiṇī* shows that additional new imposts were levied during the reigns of Śaṁkaravarman, Diddā, Saṁgrāmarāja, Ananta, Harṣa, Sussala and Jayasiṁha. We are specifically told by Kalhaṇa that Mahattama Ānanda levied fresh fines called *maṅgaladaṇḍa* during the reign of Jayasimha.[47]

42. *CII*, iv, pp. 101 and 108.
43. *On Yuan Chwang'. Travels*, ed. Watters, i, p. 176.
44. Elliot and Dowson, Hist. of Ind., i, pp. 85-86.
45. *Op. cit.*, p. 243.
46. *Rājanītiratnākara*, ed. K.P. Jayaswal, ch. xii, p. 55 (2nd ed.).
47. *Rājataraṅgiṇī*, ed. Stein, VIII. 565-568.

Inscriptions indicate the extent of fresh charges on land and its products. A comparative study of the Candella inscriptions would reveal that additional levies were collected from subjects from time to time. From the two copper-plates of Paramārdīdeva, dated A.D. 1171 and A.D. 1178, we learn that the donees were not only entitled to such taxes and imposts as *bhāga*, *bhoga*, *hiraṇya*, *śulka*, mines, minerals, iron, but also to levies on animals, deer, birds, fish, agricultural products like flax, hemp plant, sugarcane, cotton, mangoes, forests, pasture lands cultivated by the owner or others and imposts on anything sold.[48] The Rajor inscription of Mathanadeva and the Arthuna inscription of Chāmuṇḍarāja also give a comparatively longer list of taxes and imposts than we come across usually in inscriptions. Of all inscriptions between 600 and 1200 A.D. probably the longest list of revenues and taxes derived from land is preserved in a copper-plate of the Caulukya king Bhīma II, dated A.D. 1230. According to its editor, G. Būhler, we come across the following levies on fruits and plants : *methī*, *āmlā*, *veherā*, *kaṇabhṛtapatra*, *mañjiṣthā*, *hiṅga*, *trapuka*, *hiṅgulla*, *śrīkhaṇḍa*, *karpūra*, *mālapatra*, *jāiphala*, *jāivatrī*, *nārikela*, *haraḍā*, sugarcane, *guggula*, *maricha*, *marūmāṁsa*, *vathaloha*, *cīyāhala*, *kharjura*, etc.[49]

The Smṛtis of Gupta times refer to levies on different agricultural products viz., *dhānya*, *vṛkṣa*, *mūla*, *tṛṇa*, *phala*, but each one of these terms is very general and might cover several items. It would be therefore hazardous to compare the Smṛti list with the list of specific products in early medieval inscriptions and thus discern new taxes. Yet, a few taxes noticeable after A.D. 600 seem to have been fresh impositions in contrast to Gupta times. These new taxes are *khalabhikṣā*, mentioned in inscriptions of Mathanadeva and the Caulukya kings, *ārāmodbhidyadyāna* and *vāṭikā* or taxes on groves of trees and

48. *IA*, xxv, p. 207; *EI*, xx, pp. 130-31. The enumerated taxes : in the Ichchhnawar plates dated pp. 1171 are : *bhāgabhoga paśu hirṇya kara śulk ādi—.arvvam asmai samıpanetavyam* ı *Tad enam asye grāmaṁ samandira—prākāraṁ sanirggama—praveśaṁ sasarvvāśam* ϵ *ksukarpasakusumasaṇāmrādibhūruham-savanakhaninidhānaṁ salohādyākaraṁ sagokulaṁ sapaśumṛgavihaṅgam—jalacaram aparairapisīmāntaraggatair vastubhiḥsahitaṁ savāhyābhyantarādāyam bhuñjānasya karṣataḥ karṣayats dānādhānavikrayaṁ vā kuruvato.*

49. *IA*, vi, p. 202.

gardens mentioned in the Kalacuri and Gāhaḍavāla inscriptions and taxes *saivāla* or moss mentioned in inscriptions of Devavarman Candella. Two other indications of the increasing taxes and cesses after A.D. 600 may be also considered. R.S. Sharma rightly points out that such dues as the *akṣapaṭalaprastha* and *pratihāraprastha* in the Gāhaḍavāla landgrants, *rājakulābhāvya* in Ramgank copper-plate of Iśvaraghoṣa, *talarābhāvya*, *selahastābhāvya* and *valādhipābhāvya* in the Cāhamāna and Caulukya inscriptions, *paṭṭakilādāya* in the Jabalpur inscription of Jayasiṁha are unknown to Gupta and pre-Gupta ages.[50] These levies were so called because they might have been collected by the above-mentioned officials either in the whole kingdom or in their respective localities. It is also interesting to note that the list of officials in inscriptions become longer in the post-Gupta period. The long list of officials in inscriptions of small kings like Iśvaraghoṣa in Bengal and Saṁgrāmagupta in north Bihar tend to show that the machinery of government was becoming more complex. The demands of the administration or welfare projects had increased so much that the Kalacuri king Jayasiṁha had to impose a tax called *kalyāṇadhana* some time before 1175 A.D.[51]

As compared to Maurya and Gupta times, *bali* and *kara* ceased to be separate taxes in early medieval India. Commentators of Manu identify *kara* with *bhāga* or king's due share of grain and with other forms of taxes.[52] Apart from these commentaries, the views of Abhayatilaka Gaṇi is worthy of consideration. Commenting on the use of the word *karaḥ* in Hemachandra's *Dvyāśraya* (III, verse 18) he states that it was the share due to the king and payable by one who enjoys the fruits of the royal agricultural lands and pastures.[53] Elsewhere he says that the *kara* was paid by cultivators during the harvesting season in kind.

50. *Indian Feudalism* : 300-1200, Calcutta, 1965, pp. 188-190.

50. *CII*, iv, p. 343 l. 13.

52. Medhātithi on Manu VIII. 347, Kullūkabhaṭṭa on the same verse of Manu says that *kara* means realisation of contribution from villager either every month or in the months of *Bhādra* and Pauṣa evey year. Bute on Manu VII. 137 he observes that it was levied by the king on vegetables, plants, sale and purchase of goods etc.

53. *Kṛṣi paśucāraṇādikṛta rājakīya bhūmyupobhogahetuko rājagrāhyo bhāgaḥ.*

Neither literature nor inscriptions of early medieval India mention the prices of articles, or provide statistics of agricultural production and population.[54] But some conjectures may be made regarding the incidence of taxes and increasing burdens on the community. Any fresh tax is bound to increase the price of goods, and there was a number of new taxes in the post-Gupta period, as we have seen earlier. On the evidence of inscriptions, sugarcane, cotton, flax, betelnuts, which were not subjected to payment of taxes in Gupta times, became sources of revenue to the state after A.D. 600. We have also seen that additional taxes were levied on wheat by the Cāhamāna kings. As demand for wheat is inelastic in Rajputana, its price must have risen by the full amount of tax, and the incidence fell on the consumers.

In spite of increasing taxes and rising prices we do not know of any recorded instance of the revolt of the people in early medieval India except in Kashmir. Kalhaṇa tells us that several times brāhmaṇas resorted to fasts against the exactions and taxes imposed by Kashmiri kings.[55] Brāhmaṇas of other parts of India did not take the leadership of the oppressed subjects. Should we argue that influential and enterprising brāhmaṇas were silenced by numerous land grants and offers of big posts ? Those belonging to other three castes, *antyajas* and untouchables were not high-up in the social ladder and bureaucratic frame. People of one kingdom probably welcomed occasional raids made by the princes of the neighbouring kingdom. The mass of people remained apathetic to such raids and showed hardly any noteworthy concern about the Turko-Afghan invasions, because, they might have thought that the establishment of a new power may lessen the burden of taxes and bring greater relief.

54. Excepting Kashmir, where Kalhaṇa introduces to us the price of some important articles like rice and occasional references to the number of people affected by mishaps.

55. Mazumdar, B. P., *Socio-economic history of N. India*, Calcutta, 1960, pp. 238-39.

III

ASPECTS OF LAND REVENUE ADMINISTRATION IN THE MUGHAL PERIOD

Qeyamuddin Ahmad

The present paper covers the period from the reign of Akbar to Aurangzeb, and it discusses the land revenue system prevalent in the Northern *Ṣubāhs* of the Mughal Empire. The Maratha revenue system as also those prevailing in the states of Rajputana, although important by themselves, are not included here. Sher Shah's system however, has been referred to briefly as the starting point for Akbar's reforms.

An important source for the study of land revenue in the Mughal period is the *Āīn-i-Akbari*, which is supplemented by administrative manuals and contemporary documents. However, the understanding of many aspects of the Mughal land revenue system is not as easy as it appears to be. The description in the *Āīn* and the other relevant sources is sometimes highly technical, and it assumes in the reader a degree of familiarity with the working details which is not always possible. But in spite of some of these limitations the general picture of the period is a little clearer and fuller. We have information available not only on assessment, share and collection but also on such important points as medium of payment, agency for collection, methods of relief in times of famines, attitude of the state towards the peasants and the ownership of agricultural land, etc.

1. *Methods of Assessment*

Before the implementation of what is described as the *ẓabṭ* system by Sher Shah there were two well-established methods of assessment: (i) *ghalla bakhshī* or crop-sharing and (ii) *muqṭa'ī* or compounding. Both systems continued in Mughal times. The system of crop-sharing was in vogue from ancient times. It obviated the necessity of assessment as a separate process and combined the assessment and collection in one stage. The *Aīn*[1] describes the following different varieties of crop-sharing system; i. "*baṭāī,* also called *bhāolī*; the crops are reaped and stacked and divided by agreement in the presence of the parties", ii. *khet baṭāī,* "when they divide the fields after they are sown" (but before harvesting), iii. *lāng baṭāī*; "after cutting the grain, they form it in heaps and divide it among themselves, and each takes his share home to clean it and turn it to profit". Saran[2] makes it appear that the cleaning or the separating of the chaff was done before division, but this is not borne out by the text of the *Aīn,* as given above.

Compounding was described by Moreland[3] as a system under which "a peasant compounded for his liability to the king by fixed payment for lease to occupy a certain area and grow whatever crop he chose." He is of the opinion that as a system it did not prevail before Aurangzeb's reign but admits that it might be much older.

Along with these different varieties of the crop-sharing system described above, and, as a matter of fact, just before these the *Aīn* describes another method which it designates as *kankūt*, and explains it in these words, "*kan* in the Hindi language signifies grain, and *kut*, estimate. The whole land is taken either by actual mensuration or by pacing it, and the standing crops estimated in the balance of inspection...if any doubts arise, the crops should be cut and estimated in three lot, the good, the middling and the inferior and the hesitation removed."[4]

Saran asserts that the *kankūt* should not be taken as a sub-division of the sharing system, for it refers to measurement which was never a feature of any sub-division of the sharing system.[5] He equates it with the *nasaq* system, which was established by Shihabuddin Khan in the *Khaliṣa* lands in the 13th regnal year, and also with what Moreland describes as the com-

1. *Aīn-i-Akbarī*, Eng. tr., Col. H. S. Jarrett, ii, p. 44.
2. P. Saran, *The Provincial Government of the Mughals*, Allahabad, 1941, p. 301.
3. "Sher Shah's Revenue System", *JRAS*, 1926, p. 449.
4. *Aīn*, ii, p. 44.
5. Saran, *op. cit.*, p. 301 fn. 1.

pounding system. Saran further suggests that the system described as *muqṯa'ī* in the *Aīn* was identical with this *kankūt*.

There were also some other forms of summary assessment, called *hast-o-būd*. In the Deccan, for instance, the number of ploughs was counted and assessed according to rates fixed for the different localities. Mention may also be made of the system described in some places in the *Aīn* as *nasaq*. Saran, as pointed out, equates it with *kankūt*. Moreland describes it as a system under which the amount of the revenue may be fixed by agreement with the headman or zamindar of a village or a *pargana* who in his turn distributed the amount among the individual peasants. He calls it group assessment and thinks it to be an alternative, if not opposite, method to that of *ẓabṯ* or measurement.

Irfan Habib[1] rightly points out that the *nasaq* was not an independent method of assessment, but a "handmaid" of other methods, of both sharing and measurement. Its essential feature was that there was no periodic assessment. The initial assessment once made, whether by measurement or by appraisement, was used subsequently.

Reforms in the Land Revenue Administration by Akbar.

According to the *Aīn* the systems of *ghalla bakhshī* was replaced by the *ẓabṯ* during the reigns of Sher Shah and Islam Shah. The characteristic feature of the *ẓabṯ* was the measurement of land and the fixing of the *rai'* or schedule of crop-rates. The cultivable land was divided into three categories of good, middling and bad; the standard yield, per *bigha*, (or unit of area) of all the three categories was added up and an average struck by dividing it by three, and finally 1/3 of this average, *stated in grain*, was fixed as the state demand' called the *rai'*. For vegetables and some other produce cash rates were fixed. The state demand, although stated in grain, was commuted according to a price list into cash rates known as *dastūrs* or *dastūr-ul-'amals*. The system continued during the early years of Akbar's reign, and he accepted the crop-rates sanctioned by Sher Shah. But it proved unworkable owing to the difficulties in the timely

1. I. Habib, *The Agrarian System of Mughal India*, Bombay, 1963, pp. 215, 218.

fixing of the cash rates for the different parts of the kingdom each year. The *Aīn*[1] states that the prices for the different crops were reported annually, from all over the kingdom, to the Emperor who looked into them and approved the *dastūrs*. This caused inordinate delay, and Abul Fazl admits that "much distress used to occur."

To remove this difficulty Muzaffar Khan and Todarmal were directed in the 11th regnal year to undertake surveys of land and to obtain the revenue statistics from the Qānūngoes, who prepared the schedule of crop-yields for their respective *parganas* or areas, showing the demand on each crop, stated in grain, as 1/3 of the average produce convertible into cash. This was the first change introduced by Akbar. In the beginning there seems to have been a uniform price list based probably on the rates prevailing in the Imperial Camp, but subsequently it became necessary to take account of the local prices, on which the state demand came to be based. This system continued till the adoption of the *Aīn-i-Dahsāla* when it had to be abandoned on account of more or less the same reasons which led to the first change by Akbar.

The *Aīn-i-Dahsāla* was the final remedy adopted by Akbar in his 24th regnal year. Its distinctive feature was that the demand was fixed in cash, thus removing the necessity of annual commutations and the consequential delays and uncertainties. Moreland is of the opinion that the new rates were the average of those prevailing in the last ten years, but he admits that this cannot be checked arithmetically[2]. Irfan Habib, however, rightly draws attention to a passage in the *Akbarnāma* that "the essence of this innovation is that having ascertained the ten years' state (*ḥāl-i-dah-sāla*) of every *pargana* in regard to the categories of cultivation and levels of prices, they fixed the tenth part thereof as the annual revenue."[3] Since information on area, productivity and prices was called for "what seems to have been done was to work out the crop-rates retrospectively for a locality each year and then simultaneously prepare a parallel schedule of prices, so that cash revenue rates for each of the pre-

1. *Aīn*, ii, p. 88.
2. Moreland, W. H., *The Agrarian System of Muslim India*, Cambridge, 1929; App. E.
3. Habib, *op. cit.*, p. 206.

vious year could be determined."[1] It must have been a difficult task to collect all the data, and the *Aīn* states that the rates for the immediately preceding five years were based on *taḥqīq* (research), while those of the other five years obtained orally from truthful men.

An exception was made in regard to certain cash crops such as indigo, poppy, *pān* and turmeric; their rates were fixed on the basis of certain good years of harvest.[2]

Reform in the Instrument and Unit of Measurement.

According to the *Aīn* up to the 31st regnal year the standard unit of measuring land was the *Sikandrī gaz*, which was equal to (the diametres of) 41½ *iskandris* (a bronze coin of the Lodi period). Humayun ordered the length to be made equal to 42 *iskandrīs* or 32 digits. Under Akbar while the *Akbarshāhī gaz* of 46 digits was in use for measuring clothes, cultivable land and buildings were measured only by the *Sikandrī gaz.*[3] In the 31st year His Majesty "seeing that the variety of measure was a source of inconvenience to his subjects and regarding it as subservient only to the dishonest."[4] abolished it, and brought a medium *gaz* of 41 digits into general use. It was named the *Ilāhī gaz* and was used for all purposes.

The *ṯanāb* or the instrument of measurement was a "measure of hempen rope twisted which became shorter or longer according to the dryness or moisture of the atmosphere." In the 19th year a new *jarīb* made of bamboo[5] joined by iron rings was introduced. It was not subject to variation by atmospheric conditions and "relief to the public was felt everywhere, while the hand of dishonest greed was shortened."[6] One

1. *Ibid.*

2. *Aīn*, ii, p. 65. The exact meaning of this portion of the *Aīn's* text is not quite clear, and there is some discrepancy about the text in the earlier and standard copies of the mss. For a detailed discussion see Moreland, *op. cit.*, App. E. and Ḥabib, *op. cit.*, p. 207 fn. 50.

3. *Aīn*, ii, p. 61.

4. *Ibid.*

5. According to a glossary of Administrative Terms compiled in the late 18th century the length of the bamboo was equal to 5 hands of the local Qazi

6. *Aīn*, ii, p. 62.

bigha was sub-divided into 20 *biswas*, each of which was divided into 20 *biswansas*. *No revenue was required (from lands) up to* 9 *biswansa, but ten biswansas was counted as one biswa*[1] (for levy of revenue ?).

Classification of Lands

Land was classified into the following categories on the basis of continuity of cultivation. i. *polaj* or land under annual cultivations for different crops in succession, ii. *parauti* or land left out of cultivation for sometime to let it recuperate its fertility, iii. *chāchar*, or land that had lain fallow for 3-4 years, iv. *banjar* or land uncultivated for five years or more. The first two categories of land were divided into good, middling and bad, and after determining the average produce 1/3 was charged as the state demand,[2] as explained above. In regard to the 3rd and 4th categories the government's policy was to charge a light amount in the beginning and to increase it gradually until in five years the standard rate was levied. Thus, the *chachar* land when brought under cultivation was charged at 2/5 of the standard rate, then 3/5, then 4/5 (there is no mention of the 4th year); until in five years the full rate was realised.[3] For the *banjar* land one or two seers of grain per bigha was charged in the 1st year, five seers in the 2nd year, 1/6 of the produce in the 3rd year and 1/4 of the produce in the 4th year.[4] Incentive was also given to the cultivation of high grade crops by remitting 1/4 of the usual assessment in the first year.[5]

The system described above prevailed generally in the whole of Northern India, comprising the *Ṣubāhs* of Lahore, Agra, Delhi, Allahabad, Awadh, Malwa and parts of Bihar. Different systems, mostly being variations of the sharing system, prevailed in some of the other provinces. In Bengal, for instance, the *nasaq* was widely prevalent. Even within the areas where the above-mentioned *ẓabṭ* system prevailed it is not

1. *Ibid.*
2. *Ibid.*, p. 63.
3. *Ibid.*, p. 67.
4. In the 3rd. year an additional levy of 5% and 1 *dām*, per *bigha*, was levied, (*ibid*. p. 68).
5. *Āin*, ii, p. 45.

possible to assert that the *aīn-i-dahsāla* with cash rates prevailed exclusively. It is laid down that the *'amalguzār* should let the peasant have a choice in regard to assessment either by *nasaq* or by measurement.[1] Further, he could also use the *kankut* or the sharing system. This was the position in 1596 at the time of compilation of the *Aīn*. No further changes are recorded either for the reign of Akbar or his successors in the 17th century. But it has to be remembered that our information for the last decade of Akbar's reign is comparatively scanty, and nothing even remotely comparable to the *Aīn* exists for the subsequent period.

The Farmans of Aurangzeb

We have the two well-known *Farmāns* of Aurangzeb addressed to Rashikdas and Muhammad Hashim.[2] These were discovered by J. N. Sarkar on the folio of a Persian ms. in the then Royal Library of Berlin and published by him along with an English translation in the *Journal of Asiatic Society of Bengal*, 1906. The *Farmān* addressed to Muhammad Hashim is accompanied by a commentary amplifying the meaning of the original text, clausewise. Although addressed to individual officers the *Farmāns* are the prototypes of similar ones sent to the officers of other provinces. Both are fairly long documents containing 15 and 18 clauses respectively, besides the commentary. The instructions contained in them were expected to be followed by the officers of both the Crownland and the jagir lands. In fact one clause asks the addressees to report on the *'āmils* of those *jāgīrdārs* who were not following them so that they could be punished. The preamble to the Rasikdas *Farmān* describes the prevailing methods of assessment as follows : "The assessors of the *parganas* of the Imperial dominions assess the *jama'* of most of the villages of the *pargana* in the beginning of the year keeping in view the revenue of the *sāl-i-kāmil* (the year of maximum revenue) and the previous year and the cultivable area and the capacity of the peasantry and other peculiarities ; and if the peasants of some of the villages do not agree

1. *Ibid.*, p. 44.

2. *JASB*, June 1906, Irfan Habib mentions another copy of the first one in the British Museum in which the name is replaced by Mir Muiz, the Diwan of Bihar—Habib, *op. cit.*, p. 222 fn. 17.

to this procedure they assess the *jama'* at the time of the ripening of the crop by the method of *jarīb* or *kankūt*. And in some of the villages whose cultivators and peasants they know to be in distress and indigent they enforce the method of Crop-sharing at half or a third part or two fifths more or less (as revenue)."[1]

On the basis of these *Farmāns* Moreland argues that Akbar's system, whose keynote was the measurement of land, was allowed to fall into disuse, without any formal revocation. He goes on to argue that Akbar's system required an energetic and watchful staff and an able monarch to supervise its working. The group assessment was a simpler method, the revenue officers were familiar with it and perhaps preferred it, for it gave them greater opportunities for illegal gratifications, and so the *ẕabṯ* system was allowed to lapse. But this argument is not quite convincing. It makes too much of the fact that the group assessment and sharing prevailed side by side with the *ẕabṯ*. But these methods prevailed simultaneously in the time of Akbar also. It is true that with the decline in the powers of the Imperial government in the 17th century and the consequential slackness in administration there was a gradual reversal to the rather summary methods of assessment. But the *ẕabṯ* system continued in its essentials throughout the 17th century: it co-existed along with the other methods. The relative preponderance of one or the other in a particular area or particular period cannot be determined exactly on the basis of the available evidence.

II. *Collection of Revenue*

The collection of revenue was a process distinct from its assessment, and it was done by a separate officer known as the *'āmil* or the *'amalguzār*. The *Aīn* instructs the *'amalguzār* to collect the revenue in an "amicable manner and extend not the hand of demand out of season."[2] The amount was collected, if necessary, in instalments according to the harvesting time. The collection for the *rabi'* crop was done during March and that of *Kharīf* in October. Aurangzeb's *Farmān* to Hashim lays down that the "time for demanding fixed revenue is the

1. Habib, *op. cit.* p. 222. I have quoted this translation by Habib in preference to the one by J. N. Sarkar.
2. *Aīn*, ii, p. 46.

harvesting of every kind of grain" (clause 8). As in the *Kharīf* season different crops were harvested at different times the revenue was often taken in instalments, not exceeding three. Because of the emphasis on collecting the revenue while the crop was standing some of the collectors prevented the peasants from cutting their crop until the revenue was paid. Two administrative manuals of the period of Aurangzeb prescribe this coercive method to the collectors.

The collected amount was deposited in the state treasury by the *'āmils*. The peasants were also permitted and even encouraged to pay their revenues directly. The Treasurer or the *foṭadār* was instructed to give them official receipts for all such payments.[1] He was also instructed to get an endorsement on his register from the *patwārī* (village accountant) to establish the amount of payment. Todarmal's recommendation, as contained in a rare copy of the *Akbarnāma* in the British Museum,[2] also refers to this point. Article 6 of the recommendations allows a time limit to loyal and upright peasants to deposit their revenue personally and obtain receipts for them. According to article 9 even when the revenue was paid through *'āmils* the receipts were to be given to the peasant, not to the *'āmil*. It was the responsibility of the *'āmil* to see that the peasant got his receipt, for if the peasant complained (about the receipt or the arrear of revenue?) "the *'āmils* will not be heard." It is evident that due precautions were taken to protect the simple peasants from bureaucratic harassments and out-right embezzlement.

No revenue was collected from lands donated for *sarais* or turned into cemeteries.[3] The *'āmils* were also authorised to grant remission in cases where "non-preventible calamities overtake a sown field." In such cases the relevant rules were constructed in such a manner as to give the maximum advantage to the peasant.[4]

1. *Ibid.*, p. 49.

2. Habib refers to this copy (p. 418).. In his opinion it is the draft of the work. It contains the full text of Todarmal's recommendations and Akbar's comments on it which is not present in the other copies.

3. *Farmān* to Muhammad Hashim, Clause 15.

4. Vide *infra*, p. 50.

III. *Medium of Payment.*

Although the *ẓabṭ* system, which prevailed in the heartland of the Empire, prescribed payment of revenue in cash, the *'āmils* were instructed not to be rigid about the medium of payment. "Let him not make it a practice of taking only in cash payments, but also in kind."[1] Kashmir had a peculiar method of payment under which rice was collected in terms of "ass-loads". Later, an attempt was made to substitute it by cash payment, but the practice of crop-sharing was very old and Akbar forbade collection in cash. In Orissa, according to the testimony of some European travellers, coins were scrace and cowries were in use, but it is not definitely known whether these were used as a medium of paying revenue. Jahangir refers[2] to the practice in Sylhet area of the peasants giving away their children for being castrated in satisfaction of State demand, but it is not clear whether it was a normal practice or, as is more likely, an extreme case of hardship. In the reign of Akbar the demand was stated in *dāms*, and *jitals*, which were copper coins, but payment could be made in any coin whether of gold or silver. The *Aīn*[3] instructs the Treasurer to "receive from the cultivators any kind of *mohurs*, rupees or copper that he may bring and not demand any particular coin." No discount was to be charged on the current coins except when the coin was deficient in weight, in which case only the equivalent of the deficiency in weight was to be taken. Coins of the former periods were treated as bullion. The Rashikdas *Farmān* (clause 8) lays down the rules in regard to the coins which were to be received in the State treasuries in payment of land revenue. There was an emphasis on payment in *sicca* rupees or current rupees. "Order the *foṭadār* only to receive Alamgir coins" (clause 8), but if these were not available then rupees of Shahjahan's reign were to be accepted and a *Sikka abwāb* (discount for exchange) was to be charged upon them. Coins of short weight were not to be received, but if it was found that collection would be delayed if defective coins are returned the *foṭadārs* were instructed "to take from the ryots the exact and

1. *Aīn*, ii, p. 44.
2. *Tuzuk*, pp. 71-2.
3. *Aīn*, ii, p. 49.

true discount for changing them into current coins, and immediately so change them." (clause 8).

IV. *Assignments.*

All land was divided into two broad and basic categories of *Khaliṣa* land and assigned lands. The latter was also known as *tuyūl*, *jāgīr* or *iqṭā'*. The difference between the two was that the revenue administration of the former was directly under government departments while the revenue of the latter was assigned by the Emperor to different categories of his officers and subjects.

Moreland was the earliest important writer on the subject to point out that the common rendering of assigned lands as fiefs was wrong. Fiefs have a peculiar feudal connotation which is not to be found in the *jāgīr* lands of the Mughal period. He rightly points out that the chief feature of the system was to "set aside particular items of recurring revenue to meet particular items of recurring expenditure, usually, but not invariably, the salaries and expenses of the Imperial Service."[1] He accordingly calls it the system of assignment of revenue or just assignment, which is nearer the correct position. Only the revenues of the lands were assigned to the holders, but they had no other administrative functions. In certain cases the assignments carried special administrative jurisdictions. For instance, the adjacent areas of important forts, such as Rohtas, were usually assigned to the commander of the fort.

There were two kinds of assignments, (i) service assignments and (ii) charitable or non-conditional grants. The former was conditional upon the performance of certain duties. Such grants were made in terms of *dāms*, the latter were without any conditions and were granted in terms of area of land.

It was essential for the working of service assignments that the government should have detailed statistics of the revenue yield of the different areas so that the correct area of land, worth the required revenue yield, might be assigned to the officers corresponding to their salary. The *jama'* statistics, *jama'-i-raqmī* as they were called, which existed in the early years of Akbar's reign, had been inherited from the Sur regime. They

1. Moreland, *op. cit.*, p. 93.

were found to be grossly inflated. As a result the *jāgīrs* assigned to the different officers were found to yield generally much less than their face value. A problem of great perplexity, it constantly engaged the attention of Akbar. Several attempts were made first through the Qānūngoes and then by directly supervised survey of land to collect a more reliable estimate of the revenue yield of the various areas. Some improvement was made, but the malady was never fully cured. On the contrary, we get numerous references to the complaints by the assignees.[1] Irfan Habib on the basis of a large number of 17th century documents shows that under Shahjahan a new method of month-ratio was worked out to meet this difficulty.[2] The difference between the actual and nominal yields of assigned lands was accepted as an unavoidable evil. Under the new arrangement *jāgīrs* were graded into different classes depending on the ratio between their actual and nominal yield. Thus, a *jāgīr* whose revenue corresponded fully to its nominal value was a first class *jāgīr*—it was called *dwazdah māha* (12 monthly); one whose ratio was 50% was called *shash māha*, (6 monthly) and so on.

A more important question relates to the assessment and collection of revenue by the *jāgīrdārs* and the extent of the control exercised over them by the Imperial government. Although the assignee was theoretically entitled to assess and collect the revenue of his *jāgīr* the former right was much curbed by requiring him to conform to imperial regulations. During the early years of Akbar's reign it was required that the *jāgīrdārs* should collect the revenues in accordance with the cash rates sanctioned by the Court.[3] Todarmal's recommendations contain an article requiring all collection either by government officers or *jāgīrdār's* employees to be according to the sanctioned rates. Any excess collection over that was not only to be recovered but punished for. Finally, we have the Rashikdas *Farmān* which orders the addressee to "report the names of those among the *amīns* and *karōrīs* of the *jāgīrdārs*, who have served with uprightness...But if any have acted in the opposite manner report the

1 *Early Travels in India*, ed. W. Foster, London, 1927 pp. 91, 93.

2. Habib, *op. cit.*, p. 264 fn. 30.

3 Moreland, *op. cit.*, pp. 91-92, Habib, *op. cit.*, p. 273.

fact to the Emperor that they may be dimissed from service, put on their defence and explanation (of their conduct) and receive the punishment of their irregular acts" (clause 12).

This, however, does not mean that the imperial control was always effectively exercised. Every *jāgīrdār* was anxious to collect a little more than the sanctioned amount and he very often succeeded in doing so. Sometimes he was caught, but such occasions were, perhaps, very few. Moreland aptly sums up the position thus, "the peasants under an assignee would ordinarily pay as much as, but not much more than, peasants in the reserved areas."[1]

It is not clear whether the *jāgīrdārs* enjoyed any option in choosing out of the various methods of assessment.

Not much direct information is available regarding the agency for collection in the *jāgīr* lands. However, it is obvious that many of the *jāgīrdārs*, partly because of the departmental transfers, were away from their *jāgīrs*. The only practical course left to them was to employ local agents or *gumāshtās* for collecting the revenues. Owing to their limited resources the *jāgīrdārs* could not have employed the same set of officers as employed in the *Khaliṣa* lands, but their agents too often bore the same designations.[2] Very often the functions of the different officers were combined. The *jagīrdārs* also took caution money (*qabẓ*) from their agents as security for full payment of the amount of revenue. From this the next step was *ijārā* or farming out the collection of revenue. The practice was for obvious reasons very harmful to the peasants.

The Suyūrghāls.

Another class of land of which the revenue was assigned was known as *suyūrghāl*. The *Aīn* describes the system in the following words. "His Majesty from his desire to promote rank distinctions, confers lands and subsistence allowances on the following four classes of men, first on enquirers after wisdom who have withdrawn from all worldly occupations, and make no distinction between night and daytime in searching after true knowledge; secondly on such as toil and practice self-

1. Moreland, *op. cit.*, p. 92.
2. *Baharistan-i-Ghaibi*, Eng. tr. Borah, ii, pp. 566-68.

denial..thirdly, on such as are weak and poor and have no strength for enquiry; fourthly, on honourable men of gentle birth who for want of knowledge are unable to provide for themselves by taking up a trade."[1] The cash allowance was known as *waẓīfa* or *yaumīa*, and the land grants as *milk*, *madad-i-ma'āsh* or *a'imma*. Actually, the grants were not confined only to these classes of people. Women, although not clearly excluded in the above mentioned classification, also received such grants. A document of the early 19th century belonging to Mir Nayyar Ali Saheb of Purnea shows that one of his ancestor received a grant of land and a cash allowance because as a physician he gave free treatment to the poor and the indigent. Hindu divines also received such grants.[2]

These grants were essentially of a charitable nature. The recipient was not called upon to perform any duty although the vague and pious wish was invariably expressed that having availed himself of the income the grantee shall pray for the prosperity and the continuity of the kingdom. Jahangir aptly calls them the Army of Prayers and is said to have remarked that they were as essential as the real army.[3] Sometimes conditional *madad-i-ma'āsh* grants were also made. For instance, there are a number of *Sanads* of appointments of *qāẓis* in *pargana* Mahsi (district Champaran) which show that they received ex-officio *madad-i-ma'āsh* grants.[4]

All such *Farmāns* and *Sanads* had a standardised phraseology, which came to be adopted right from the early years of Akbar's reign. Under these grants the revenue of a specified area was assigned to the grantee, who was exempted from the payment of the large number of *abwābs*, or customary dues, which were enumerated. This was a concession of considerable economic significance for it put the grantee in a favoured position as compared to the general cultivator who had to pay all the *abwābs*, even if illegally. If the land granted was *banjar* the grantee could develop it and utilise its produce without paying any revenue to the government. In the earlier period—as a

1. *Āīn-i-Akbarī*, Eng. tr. Blochmann, Calcutta, 1873, i, p. 268.
2. *Journal of Pakistan Historical Society*, v-vi, pp. 254, 55-65.
3. *Tuzuk*, p. 5.
4. See my article, "A Note on Pargana Mehsi" *JBRS*, xliv, Pts. III-IV.

corollary to the policy of extending the area of cultivation—grants were often made in such a way that one half of the land was uncultivated and the other half cultivated. There was no limit to the area under such grants, which ranged from 5 to 1500 *bīghas* or even more. Nor was there any specification about the officers or persons who could make such grants. Apart from the emperors, princes, and *ṣubahdārs*, other high dignitaries as well as *jāgīrdārs* gave such grants (in the last two cases, of course, within their own areas). Technically these were not *madad-i-ma'āsh* grants, but they served the same purpose of providing livelihood and subsistence.

Some *Farmāns* of Akbar's reign make a distinction between *khud kāshta* (cultivated by the grantee himself) and *ra'iyati* lands (peasant-held land). The grantee was forbidden from interfering with the latter's occupancy right. The origin of the distinction might perhaps be traced to the practice, referred to above, of apportioning half of the granted land as uncultivated. When this was brought under cultivation by the grantee it was known as *khud kāsht.* The grantee did not have any proprietory right over the land. Documents show that the grantee had to pay *ḥaqq-i-milkiat* (a tax to the owner) to the "owner."[1] The owner's hostility often forced the grantee to seek a grant elsewhere.[2] This *ḥaqq-i-milkiat* related to a share in produce, not proprietory right.

A *Farmān* of Aurangzeb defines *madad-i-ma'āsh* as *a'āriyat* or something held on loan.[3] But instances are known of the holder selling away or leasing his right of collection, as distinct from ownership, to someone.

Grants were made both for the lifetime of the grantee as well as in heredity—in the latter case descending down to the successors of not only the sons but also the daughters of the grantee. But the overriding right of the king always remained intact. Each new incumbent had to get his right confirmed. The king's right to resume, revoke and modify all such grants existed not only in theory but was frequently exercised. During the early period there was no definite rule about the inheritance

1. Habib, *op. cit.*, p. 301.
2. *Ibid.*
3. *Ibid.*, p. 303.

to such lands. The heirs had to apply afresh, and even then sometime only a portion of the original grant was renewed. But in Aurangzeb's reign an order was passed declaring all such lands as inheritable. Even then a distinction was made that as the land was held in *a'āriyat*, not in ownership, its inheritance was to be governed by administrative laws and not the *Shara'* as it related to normal matters of inheritance.[1]

Not much accurate information is available about the extent of such lands and the amount of the revenue thus assigned. The *Aīn* mentions certain figures in *dāms* under the heading of *suyūrghāls* in the Provincial Tables. It is not however clear whether they represent the amount of revenue thus alienated or include cash grants too. Irfan Habib computes the proportion to be around 5% in the Gangetic area and 1.8% in Lahore and Gujarat.[2] He is also of the opinion that in the early period the *madad-i-ma'āsh* holders as a class were a minor factor and did not play a significant role in the agrarian economy. But towards the end of the Mughal period, particularly in the second half of the 18th century, the position changed much. Such grants were made on an extensive scale, so that when the *Diwani* of Bengal and Bihar was conferred on the E.I. Company (1765) the English administrators found that "the revenue of one-fourth of the whole province had been transferred from State."[3] As a result much confusion and anomaly prevailed. Many persons were enjoying rent-free tenures on fictitious title deeds and forged documents.

The English therefore started a series of Land Resumption Proceedings aimed at checking the authenticity of all such title deeds and for resuming or bringing under assessment the lands not held under properly authenticated documents.[4] The methods adopted by Resumption Officers were harsh and ruthless. Hunter feels constrained to admit that "we demanded an amount of proof in support of rent free tenures which in the then uncertain state of property law they could not have produced in support of their acknowledged estate."[5]

1. *Ibid.*, p. 306.
2. *Ibid.*, p. 314.
3. Hunter, W. W., *Our Indian Mussalmans*, London, 1871, p. 182.
4. See my article, "Some Historically Valuable Persian Papers Preserved in the Muzaffarpur Collectorate," *JBRS*, xli, pp. 515-516.
5. Hunter, *op. cit.*, p. 183.

Another, though unintended, result of these proceedings was that they brought into government's possession a large number of *Farmāns* and *Sanads* of grants of land which the owners presented in support of their case. Many of the *Farmāns* and *Sanads* which are now preserved in the District and Divisional Record Rooms are part of these proceedings.

The position in regard to the work of collection in these small holdings is not clear. The majority of such grants being of a small extent the holders, obviously, could not have afforded a regular staff or a uniform method. The practice of *ijāra* (farming) or sub-leasing, which was resorted to even by bigger *jāgīrdārs*, might have been generally adopted. There are some instances in which the farmers refused to pay the stipulated amount to such grantees, and they had to get their grants transferred to some other village.[1] Many of them might have cultivated the lands themselves. In fact this might explain to some extent the growth of Muslim population in the interior areas.

V. *Methods of granting Relief to the Peasants.*

Agricultural production in medieval times, as even now to some extent, depended on a number of natural phenomena and its fortunes were linked with the vagaries of the weather. The weather affected agriculture in both ways. A succession of good harvests might well be a 'disaster' on account of the limited transport facilities and the resultant restricted market. The Rashikdas *Farmān* lists 'low prices' in the same category as decrease in produce, drought and blight.

The various methods of relief prevalent in the Mughal period aimed at, both, giving immediate relief to the peasants in times of distress and increasing the area of cultivated land. Remission of revenues and grant of cash assistance (*taqāvī*) for purchase of seeds and implements was the standard form of relief. This was provided for under all methods of assessment. Under the crop-sharing system the state shared the benefits and burdens of any fluctuation in the produce—its share automatically rose and fell with the annual output. In the *ẓabṭ* system a reduction was made in the area assessed—which was treated as *nābūd* (destroyed). A distinction was made about non-

1. Habib, *op. cit.*, p. 300.

preventible calamities occuring before or after the harvest. Remissions were granted in the case of the former, not the latter (*Farmān* to Hashim, clause 9). It was also laid down in the same *Farmān* that in lands subject to a fixed revenue remissions were to be granted for non-preventible calamities in such a way as to leave the net one half of the produce to the cultivator. The accompanying commentary amplifies and illustrates it thus "Ten maunds are produced in a field; on account of calamity six maunds only are left (safe); the net half of this (total) is five maunds; threfore you should take one maund only (as revenue) so that the net half (viz.) five maunds may be left to the ryot." It shows that the rule was meant to be observed in such a way as to give the maximum benefit to the peasant. However, actual instance of the implementation of the rule in the desired manner do not exist.

It was the practice to hold the present cultivator responsible for the dues of the previous one who might have absconded or died. But Aurangzeb passed an order in the 16th year prohibiting this practice both in the Crown land and the *jāgīrs*. Only the arrears up to the preceding year were to be recovered, older ones being written off.

Akbar continued the practice of collecting ten seers of grain from each *bīgha* of tilled land, as was the rule under Sher Shah. It was a sort of emergency tax. The grain thus collected was stored in state granaries, which were constructed in every. district.[1] The grain was used as fodder for the animals belonging to the state, but they "prove at the same time of great use for the people, for poor cultivators may receive grain for sowing purposes, or people may buy cheap grain at the time of famines."

The grant of cash assisstance to "needy husbandmen" and "peasants unable to procure the implements of tillage" are specifically recommended in the *Aīn*[2] and Aurangzeb's *Farmān*. Todarmal's recommendations suggest that loan should be given to such cultivators as did not have seed or cattle and were in generally distressed circumstances. Large-scale remissions were made in the amounts of assessed revenues in times

1. *Aīn*, i, p. 275.
2. *Ibid*, ii, p. 43.

of famines. There are numerous instances, but the most liberal one relates to the great famine of Gujarat and the Deccan in 1630-32. In the *khaliṣa* lands alone, with a total *jama'* of 80 crore *dāms*, revenue worth 70 lakhs of rupees was remitted.[1] The *jāgīrdārs* also had to grant similar remissions, for which they were compensated by grants of equivalent amount elsewhere. Thus, in the final calculaion the cost of remission in both the Crown lands and the *jāgīr* lands was borne by the state itself.

Extension of Agriculture.

Extension of agricultural land and the increase of high grade crops were the two major objectives of the agrarian policy under the Mughals. Various devices aimed at the achievement of these objectives were incorporated in the system of land revenue administration. The *Aīn* and some of the other administrative manuals repeatedly refer to the directions given to revenue officer to achieve these aims. The instruction to the *'āmil* contains, *inter alia*, the following : "He should be a friend of the agriculturist....he should assist the needy husbandmen with advances of money and recover them gradually...he should strive to bring waste land into cultivation .. he should stimulate the increase of valuable produce and remit somewhat of the assessment with a view to its augmentation."[2] The Rashikdas *Farmān* enjoins as follows : "Devise the means by which *banjar* lands may be brought under cultivation" (clause 2). It also emphasises the necessity for increasing the first rate crops. Conciliation and reassurances were to be used in an effort to bring back the absconded cultivator, the causes of their escape were to be ascertained with a view to removing them (clause 2).

Other concessions were also given. The cultivator of a *banjar* land could have his choice in regard to the method of assessment and mode of payment. If there was no *banjar* land in a village and a cultivator was willing to cultivate more land he was given land in the adjoining village.[3]

1. Lahori, *Pādshāhnāma*, I, p. 364. Irfan Habib (p. 250. n. 9) is of the view that the total *jama'* figure (80 crore *dāms*) apparently belongs to the *Khaliṣa* of the whole Empire.
2. *Aīn*, ii, pp. 43-44.
3. *Ibid*, p. 68.

Apart from such forms of direct financial relief the state also undertook some other and more basic measures, such as construction of canals, digging and repairing of tanks and wells. Shahjahan's reign is significant in this respect, but generally there is not much information on this topic. Irfan Habib is of the opinion that the main purpose of the two great canals built during Shahjahan's reign was not to provide water for the fields but to supply water for the fort at Shahjahanabad and to irrigate the gardens at Lahore. But this cannot be said of the specific orders to revenue officers regarding repair of disused wells and construction of new ones contained in the Rashikdas *Farmān* (Preamble).

Government's Attitude towards the Peasant

The Mughal government, at least during the reigns of Akbar to Aurangzeb, was a benevolent despotism. The influence of this characteristic feature is traceable in the working of its different departments, including that of the land revenue. The bulk of the state's income was derived from land revenue and the peasant was the source of that income. The significance of this position was appreciated by the rulers as well as the administrators. According to Abbas Sarwani, Sher Shah is said to have remarked, "I know well that cultivation depends on the humble peasants, for if they be ill they will produce nothing but if prosperous they will produce more." Or again, a more significant remark, "The cultivators are the source of prosperity ...if a ruler cannot protect the humble peasantry from the lawless, it is tyranny to exact revenue from them." The same sentiment is reiterated in the *Aīn* in the instructions to the different revenue officers. The preamble to the Rashikdas *Farmān* states that "the desires and the aims of the Emperor are directed to the increase of cultivation and welfare of the people at large who are the marvellous creation of and a trust from the Creator."

It is true that these admirable sentiments were not always given effect to. There is considerable information, based to some extent on the observations of European travellers (Pelsaert, Bernier, Manucci and others) showing the impoverishment of the peasants and the workers in general. But this sort of criticism can be, and often is, overdone. Much of the distress was caused by the system of assessment which came into vogue during the latter period. The farmers with no permanent interest in the land but only collection right fleeced the peasants as much as they could.

The fundamental attitude of the government seemed to be that the peasant owed it as a duty to the state to cultivate his field and pay the revenue for it. The *Farmān* to Hashim orders that if "in spite of their being able to till and having had rainfall, they were abstaining from cultivation, you should urge and threaten them and employ force and beating..." But this general attitude was considerably modified by the practical needs of the situation. The problems under the Mughals, particularly in the 17th Century, was not scarcity of land but of peasants. A policy based on appropriation of practically all his surplus produce or of impoverishing him completely would have been self-defeating.

IV

EXPERIMENTS IN LAND REVENUE ADMINISTRATION IN BENGAL (1765-1793)

V. A. Narain

The grant of Diwani to the East India Company on the payment of an annual sum of twentysix lakhs of rupees to the Mughal Emperor is the starting point of British revenue administration in the Bengal Presidency. The idea of the East India Company as Diwan had originated as early as 1758 in the form of a suggestion from the Vizier to the President of the Council at Calcutta,[1] but it materialised only on 12 August 1765 when Shah Alam, the Emperor of Delhi, assigned to the East India Company the Diwani of Bengal, Bihar and Orissa. Before the grant of the Diwani, the territorial revenue of the Company was limited to the Zamindari of Calcutta, 24 Parganas, and the assigned districts of Burdwan, Midnapur and Chittagong. These were each under the administration of a Company's servant called Resident or Chief, who acted under the general control of a Committee of Lands formed initially in 1758 to collect the revenues of the 24 Parganas.[2] The function of the Committee was probably taken over by a Collector General appointed in November, 1765 to supervise the collections of the said districts. He was answerable to the President and Council at Fort William until 1772, when the Residents or Chiefs of those districts became directly responsible to the Board of Revenue.[3]

Up to 1765, considering the extent of the territories, the problem of revenue administration had been relatively simple. But by the acquisition of the Diwani from the Mughal Emperor, the East India Company obtained in effect "the superintendency", to quote the actual words of Clive, "of all the Lands,

1. W. K. Firminger, (ed.), *The Fifth Report to the House of Commons on East India Affairs*, i. Calcutta, 1917-18, pp cliv-clv.

2. *Ibid.*, p. 4.

3. *Ibid.*

and the collection of all the Revenues of the Province of Bengal, Bahar, and Orissa."[1]

The East India Company did not immediately take upon itself the work of the actual collections of the revenue. It delegated that work to naib Diwans appointed by it. Muhammad Reza Khan in conjunction with Shitab Roy (for Bihar) and Roy Durlav : (for Orissa) looked after it. The Company contented itself with vesting the superintendence of the collections in the British Resident at the Murshidabad Darbar, who functioned under the supervision and control of the President and Council at Calcutta.

In continuing the established Indian system Clive was guided by expediency and policy. "In the infancy of the acquisition (of the diwani)", wrote Clive, "we were under the necessity of confiding in the old officers of the government from whom we were to derive our knowledge, and whom we therefore endeavoured to attract to our service by the ties of interest, until experience should render their assistance less necessary. Policy required we should pursue every step likely to conciliate the natives to our Government."[2]

This arrangement was also in accordance with the desire of the Court of Directors. They observed. "The experience we have already had in the Province of Burdwan, convinces us how unfit an Englishman is to conduct the collection of the Revenues, and follow the subtle native through all his Arts to conceal the real value of his country, to perplex and to elude the Payments. We, therefore, entirely approve of your preserving the ancient Form of Government in the upholding the Dignity of the Soubah."[3]

Under this arrangement the Company while appropriating the revenues of the provinces was relieved of the burden of administration. But it was a system which enabled the Company, to use the words of Kaye, to "gorge themselves on the

1. Cited in D. N. Banerjee, *Early Land Revenue System in Bengal and Bihar*, i, 1765-1772, Calcutta, 1936, pp. 2-3.

2. Clive to Court of Directors, 29 September, 1765 I.O. MSS Eur. E. 12 ff, 76-77 quoted in B.B. Misra *The Central Administration of the East India Company*, 1773-1834, Manchester, 1959, p. 109.

3. D. N. Banerjee, *op. cit*, pp. 8-9.

revenue leaving the responsibility."[1] Responsibility thus continued to be divorced from power until a plan of supervision was adopted in 1769.

Supervision became necessary because of the general decline in the country caused by the exercise of power without responsibility. "The native officers and farmers of revenue frequently committed acts of rapacity and oppression without any fear of punishment by Government which seldom interposed its authority so long as they satisfied its revenue demands."[2] But when in spite of rackrenting the collections did not equal the assessments, the Company felt that it had been defrauded by the naib Diwans and their Indian officials.[3] It felt it had to associate itself in a greater measure with the revenue administration.

Accordingly, in August 1769 at the instance of Richard Becher, the Resident at Murshidabad, the Select Committee appointed British Supervisors "with powers of superintending the native officers employed in collecting the revenue,[4]" and charged with the duty of enquiring into the history of the provinces and preparation of rent rolls.[5] In July 1770, at the instance of the Court of Directors, two Councils of Revenue were established, one at Murshidabad, and the other at Patna to control the work of the Supervisors, and in March 1771, a Controlling Committee of Revenue was constituted at Calcutta[6] to supervise the work of the two Provincial Councils and of the revenue officers of the 24 Parganas and the three ceded districts. But the remedy proved unavailing, and in 1771, the Company decided to assume the burden of revenue administration. The decision of the Court of Directors was communicated to the authorities in Calcutta by their letter dated 28 August, 1771 in which they announced their decision to "stand forth as Dewan.[7]"

1. Quoted in A.C. Guha *A Brief Sketch of Land Systems of Bengal and Bihar*, Calcutta, 1915, p. 4.

2. Fifth Report, *op. cit.*, p. 4.
3. *Ibid.*, pp. 4-5.
4. *Ibid.*, p. 4.
5. *Ibid.*
6. Secret Consulations, Fort William, March 7, 1771, Cited in D. N. Banerjee, *op. cit.*, pp. 120-121.
7. *Fifth Report, op. cit.*, p. 5.

The President and Council accordingly abolished the office of both the naib diwans at Murshidabad and Patna and notified their discharge by a general proclamation of 11 May 1772. They also announced the Company's determination to bring the territorial revenues under the direct management of its own servants.[1] To provide for the immediate execution of the functions previously exercised by the two naib diwans, the President and Council constituted on 14 May 1772 a Committee of Circuit and vested it with the functions formerly exercised by the two naibs. They also designated the Supervisors as Collectors, who were to be assisted by a native diwan in each district, to act jointly with the Collector who was vested with controlling authority.[2] Thus in addition to the Collectors in the several districts who were responsible to the controlling Councils of Revenue at Murshidabad and Patna, the Department consisted at that time of the Controlling Committee of Revenue at Calcutta and the newly constituted Committee of Circuit, all being responsible ultimately to the President and Council at Fort William. As the Controlling Councils stood between the President and Council on the one hand and the Collectors on the other and obstructed the regular flow of business and deprived the Government of the opportunity to get a first hand knowledge of the districts from the Collectors, the Controlling Councils of revenue were abolished and the entire establishment of the Khalsa was removed to Calcutta in September 1772 and came to be known as Board of Revenue which was to meet twice a week.[3]

The first meeting of the Board of Revenue took place on 13 October 1772, when the Controlling Committee of Revenue at Calcutta came to an end.[4] The Committee of Circuit, on the other hand, operated until February 1773 when that body also was abolished. The structure of revenue administration was thus greatly simplified. It comprised the Board of Revenue at the Presidency with Collectors in the districts, assisted in joint responsibility by the native diwans. The diwans received orders from the Roy Royan acting jointly with the Superin-

1. *Ibid.*, pp. 5-6.
2. *Ibid.*, p. 6.
3. *Ibid.*, p. 5.
4. B. B. Misra, *op. cit.*, pp. 118-119.

tending Member of the Khalsa, who was to be a member of the Supreme Council appointed in monthly rotation.

The arrangement of the several districts under Collectors, was, however, soon altered at the instance of the Court of Directors, who ordered the President and Council to recall them to the Presidency and subsititute in their place 'some other plan for making themselves acquainted with the exact value of every district.'[1] This decision of the Court of Directors was perhaps influenced by considerations of expense on civil charges, which had risen from $ 214,353 in 1765-66, the first year of the diwani, to $ 300,598 in 1769-70, the year in which the Supervisors were appointed.[2] But the Collectors instead of being removed to the Presidency were allowed to remain at the headquarters of the divisions into which the districts were grouped. The diwani provinces were in fact divided into six divisions, each under a Provincial Council which absorbed most of the Collectors removed from the districts. The divisions so established were those of Calcutta, Burdwan, Murshidabad, Dinajpur, Dacca and Patna.[3]

Five diwans were appointed by the President and Council for the five Provincial Councils, and the Roy Royan was nominated to act as diwan to the Calcutta Committee of Revenue. The vacancies caused by the recall of the Collectors were filled by naibs or deputies of the provincial diwans, who were entrusted with the superintendence of the revenue and civil justice in those districts which did not form seat of a grand division.[4] But this system did not work well. There was 'a monotonous list of large deficits, defaulting Zamindars, absconding farmer and deserting ryats.'[5] Therefore, in February 1781, the Governor General in Council abolished the Provincial Councils, but left untouched the existing apparatus of district administration. Several chiefs and Collectors of separate districts were asked to remain in their respective stations and act under a Committee of Revenue established at the Presidency with four covenanted servants of the Company.[6]

1. Home Misc. 351, f. 15, April 7, 1773, cited in B. B. Misra, *op. cit.*, p. 119.
2. *Ibid.*
3. *Fifth Report, op. cit.*, p. 8.
4. B. B. Misra, *op. cit.*, p. 121.
5. *Cambridge History of India*, v, p. 419.
6. *Fifth Report, op. cit.*, p. 10.

The system of district administration in 1781 thus "represented a conglomeration of diverse principles."[1] On the abolition of the Provincial Councils their chiefs were given the charge of Burdwan, Murshidabad, Dinajpur, Dacca and Patna, which had formed the seat of the grand divisions.[2] Other districts were placed under the charge of naibs or Indian officers of revenue who were given the powers of collection only.

This heterogeneous form of district administration soon became unacceptable to some of the Company's able and experienced servants (Shore and Stuart), who recommended that the system of 1772 should be restored and that a Company's covenanted servant should be appointed in every district with powers to administer both revenue and civil justice.[3] This was accepted by the Court of Directors, and in 1786 the district administration of the country was again vested in the convenanted servants of the Company. The Committee of Revenue, which had been established in 1781, was abolished, and in its place a Board of Revenue was set up with a member of the Supreme Council as its president and four covenanted servants as its members.[4] This system continued upto 1793.

Rents derived from lands constituted in those days "the principal source of revenue."[5] All the lands in Bengal and Bihar were considered as belonging to the crown or sovereign of the country, who claimed a right to collect rents or revenues from all of them[6] except from such lands as were appropriated to charitable and religious purposes. Being gifts from different princes, they were 'understood by the general tenor of such grants to be exempted from the payment of any rent to the sovereign.'[7]

There were, besides, other lands, 'held by grants of different kinds' which paid, 'only a fixed annual acknowledgement or rent which was generally much below the medium rate of rents in the provinces of Bengal and Bihar. These lands

1. B. B. Misra, *op. cit.*, p. 127.
2. Fifth Report, *op. cit.*, p. 10.
3. B. B. Misra, *op. cit.*, p. 128.
4. *Fifth Report*, *op. cit.*, 43.
5. *Ibid.*, p. 25.
6. D. N. Banerjee, *op. cit.*, p.11.
7. *Ibid.*

were called 'Jaghires' or 'Talooks' according as they were 'grants from the Crown to individuals' or 'grants from the Nabob or prince to individuals.[1] Jagir was an assignment by the Government of a share of the produce of a portion of land to an individual, generally for military purposes. Taluk in Bengal was a small zamindari, held by a Talukdar.

According to Verelst, who was Governor and President of Bengal from after the departure of Clive in January 1767 till December 1769, these jagirs and taluks differed in the nature of their tenure: the jagirs were sometimes granted for life only and sometimes for the life of other persons in the same family; but the taluks did 'more regularly descend to the heirs of the first grantees, than the Jaghires.'[2]

Moreover, the Rajas and Zamindars of the time, had 'certain lands, perquisites and allowances' which they used to 'hold by virtue of their offices for their support.'[3]

The revenues in respect of all lands, excluding those held by grants in the aforesaid manner were settled annually by auction by the Diwan to several Zamindars, farmers, or collectors who would hold the lands.[4]

After the acquisition of the diwani, the revenue was settled annually at a festival called Puniya, which was held at the headquarters of every district in the month of May for Bengal and in the month of September for Bihar.[5] In preparing the rent roll the Government first endeavoured to treat for the revenues of each district with Zamindars.* If however, the Zamindar would not come to an agreement with the Government an

1. *Ibid.*
2. *Ibid.*
3. *Ibid.*
4. *Ibid.*
5. *Ibid.*, p. 12.

* Hunter classifies the Zamindars into three grades : .) The old Hindu and Muslim rajas before the conquest of Bengal by Akbar in 1576; (2) the landholders who became de facto rulers of their estates in the 17th and 18th centuries enjoying high social position on the basis of custom (3) the inferior Zamindars who held the office of revenue collectors for a generation or two, and later developed a prescriptive right to the lands of which they had been revenue collectors. These formed the bulk of the class of Zamindars. W. W. Hunter (ed), *Bengal MS. Records,* (1782-1807), i, London, 1894, p. 31.

officer called amil would be appointed to superintend the collections in their joint name. He employed a number of native collectors known as tahsildars. The settlement of the districts, where there were no Zamindars, was made with contractors or farmers of revenue for the best rent which could be procured.[1]

After the general rent roll had been settled, the several Zamindars, talukadars, farmers and others made 'agreements with those of lesser degree, either with the ancient occupiers or tenants' called Ryots, or with new tenants.

Whatever the channel through which the revenues of Government passed into the public treasury, it were the raiyats who actually paid them. According to the conditions of their tenure they were called *khudkasht*, or resident cultivators with a permanent interest in the soil under their possession, and *paikāsht*, or tenants at will, with a temporary and accidental interest in the land they cultivated for transitory period.[2] The raiyats were called *hari*, *fasli* or *komar* according to the mode of their payment. The *hari* tenants held their land on fixed rates which they had to pay even when the land remained fallow. The revenue payable by a *fasli* tenant was determined by the nature of the *fasl* or crop produced in their lands. The *komar* raiyat paid in kind and gave a share of the crop as the rent of the land held. The *komar* tenure was called *bhaoli* or *batai* in Bihar. Normally the agreement of a raiyat was deemed sacred and inviolable, and he was not to be removed from the possession of his land so long as he fulfilled his obligation according to the contract.[3]

The insecurity of cultivator's, however, proceeded from the principle of farming, which governed the assessment of land revenue. Every district was arranged in parganas, which were farmed out either to the Zamindars, amils or farmers of revenue under the domination of *ijardars*, who all engaged annually to pay a stipulated sum to the Government. A Zamindar differed from an ordinary farmer in two ways. While the former engaged to pay his revenue without any security, the latter had to produce one as a necessary condition of his engage-

1. D. N. Banerjee, *op. cit.*, pp. 14-15.
2. Bengal Select Committee Proceedings July, 8, 1769, cited in Introduction to the *Fifth Report*, pp. c/xxxvi-c/xxviii.
1. B. B. Misra, *op. cit.*, p. 172.

ment. In addition, a Zamindar was entitled to a pension called *malikānā* payable to him at the rate of about 10 per cent on his lands being brought under *khās* or direct management, either from his failure to conform to his agreement, or his refusal to accept the terms offered by the Government.[1]

This mode of settlement operated to the great disadvantage of the cultivators. Although under the terms of agreement with the Government the zamindars *āmils* and farmers were required to grant *pattas* to the raiyats, they hardly conformed to this stipulation.[2] Moreover, as Richard Becher observed : "When the English received the Grant of the Dewannee their first consideration seems to have been the raising of as large sums from the country as could be collected, to answer the pressing demands from home and to defray the large Expences here. The Zamindars not being willing or able to pay the sums required, Aumils have been sent into most of the Districts ..the Aumils have no connection or natural interest in the welfare of the country where they make collections, nor have they any certainty of holding their places beyond the year : the best recommendation they can have is to pay up their *kistbundies* punctually, to which purpose they fail not to rack the country whenever they find that they cannot otherwise pay their *kists* and secure a handsome sum for themselves."[3] In the absence of a proper *hastbud*, or comparative rent-roll of fiscal units, it was impossible to protect the cultivators against extortion. In addition, the cultivators were required to pay a number of *abwabs* and *mathouts*.

The insecurity of the cultivators was further aggravated by the commercial motives of the Company, which regarded territorial revenues as "a source of investment rather than of obligation to the taxpayers."[4] Between 1766 and 1769 goods and bullion worth 56,100,000 rupees were exported by foreign companies in India against an import of bullion worth only 5,550,000 rupees.[5]

1. *Ibid.*
2. *Ibid.*
3. Bengal Select Committee Proceedings September 18, 1765 to August 16, 1765 cited in D. N. Banerjee, *op. cit.* p. 36.
4. B. B. Misra *op. cit.*, p. 175.
5. *Ibid.*

In drawing the attention of Government to the several causes of the country's decline, Becher admitted that 'since the accession of the Company to the diwani the condition of the people of this country has been worse than it was before.'[1] He, therefore, suggested a plan of supervision.[2] The great famine of 1770, however, was an irrefutable condemnation of the system, and in 1771, the Company decided to assume the burden of revenue administration.[3]

The Directors did not forward any plan for the management of revenue. The work of devising a plan and executing it devolved on Warren Hastings, who became Governor on 13 April 1772, and his Council. They were not wholly without any guidance from previous experience. In the ceded districts, as distinguished from the diwani lands, the revenue administration had been carried on directly by the British officials. Verelst, Governor, and Becher, Resident at Darbar, had made with effect from the Bengali year 1176 (1769-70) a triennial settlement of the *mālguzārī* for the districts of Rajasshahi, Birbhum and Nadia in 1769.[4] In April 1771 the leases of the old farmers in the Burdwan province had been renewed for a period of five years.[5] A triennial settlement of land revenue in the province of Bihar had also been ordered on 15 October 1771.[6] Writing to the President and Governor of Bengal on 24 May 1769, Becher had suggested a triennial settlement, to be made with persons whose interest was bound up with the welfare of the country, and had observed that the Zamindars had a more natural interest in the welfare of their districts and were naturally more likely to give encouragement to the tenants than any *āmil*.[7]

The principal features of Hastings's plan of revenue management of 14 May 1772 were the general extension of the period of assessment to five years[8] and insistence on the

1. Select Committee Proceedings 18, September 1765 to August 16, 1765 cited in D. N. Banerjee, *op. cit.*, p. 36.
2. *Ibid.*
3. D. N. Banerjee, *op. cit.*, p. 114.
4. Select Committee Proceedings, July 8, 1769.
5. D. N. Banerjee, *op. cit.*, p. 151.
6. *Ibid.*, p. 150.
7. *Fifth Report*, Introduction.
8. *Fifth Report*, *op. cit.*, p. 6.

grant of *pattas*. While the first was designed to give a sense of security to the Zamindars and farmers, the second was calculated to protect the cultivators from extortion. No change was made in the operation of farming, which the President and Council regarded as the best mode of dealing with the intricacies of the accounts and complexities of land tenures.

In forming the settlement Hastings was inclined to give preference to the Zamindars but subject to the overriding consideration that the revenue should not suffer on that account. Settlements were to be made with them only if the Zamindars agreed to enter into all the conditions of a farmer's lease and to pay the same revenues that could be expected from the farmer.[1] As Francis correctly observed, "The lands in general were put up to public auction, in which strangers were invited to bid against the proprietors, and either ousted of the possession, and management of their estates, or allowed to retain it on the footing of farmers."[2]

Not that Hastings was entirely ignorant of the advantages of a settlement with the Zamindars. He spoke of the Zamindars as having "rivetted an authority in the district, acquired an ascendency over the minds of the ryotts and ingratiated their affections" and he noted "solid advantages...expected to accrue" from "continuing the lands under the management of those who have a natural and perpetual interest in their prosperity."[3] But he was also jealous of their influence, especially of the bigger Zamindars who, according to him, had "been found to possess an influence which they have exercised to the oppression of the ryotts, the injury of Government and the interruption of the peace of the country."[4] Moreover, his desperate need for money made him quite willing to deprive the Zamindars etc. of their ancient privileges and immunities.[5]

But the purpose of raising the largest revenue possible was not fulfilled. Estates were knocked down to speculators at a revenue which, as the old Zamindars knew, the estates

1. R. B. Ramsbotham, *Studies in the Land Revenue History of Bengal, 1769-87*, London, 19 6, p. 91.
2. *Fifth Report, op. cit.*, p. ccxciv.
3. *Ibid.*, p. ccxvii.
4. *Ibid.*
5. *Ibid.*

were unable to bear. Ignorant of the real capabilities of the country and incited by the hopes of profit, speculators readily agreed for sums which were far beyond the capacity of farmers. The result was that the districts had fallen hopelessly into arrears; and chaos invaded the entire land revenue system.[1] Hastings attributed this confusion to some defects in the collecting agency, and in 1773 he decided to centralise the whole system by the creation of a Controlling Committee of Revenue at Calcutta, with six Provincial Councils subordinate to it.[2] But, the result , financially at least, was no better.

The Council now realised that it was not in fact the agency so much as the amount to be collected that was wrong. The fault lay not so much with the administrative machinery as with the method of assessment. The remissions and irrecoverable balances under the farming system exceeded two and a half million sterling.[3] The Council realised that short term settlements would never succeed administratively or financially. Therefore in 1775, the Governor General moved that the separate opinions of the members of the Council, as to the most eligible method of settling and collecting the revenues, be recorded and submitted in writing to the Court of Directors.[4]

Warren Hastings and Barwell proposed on 22 April 1775 that estates should be sold by public auction or "farmed out on leases for life, or for two joint lives, to such reasonable people as shall offer the most advantageous terms, allowing a preference to the Zamindars provided that they have attained the age of eighteen years."[5] The revenue to be paid by the purchasers was to be settled at the medium of what was actually collected in the three preceding years, with an allowance of 15 per cent for charges of collection and their profits. This revenue was to remain fixed at this rate during the life of the purchasers.[6]

The Hastings—Barwell plan, with its partial adoption of the principle of fixed settlements and its declared preference for the zamindars, did not satisfy Philip Francis who had been

1. *Ibid.*, p. ccxxv.
2. R. B. Ramsbotham, *op. cit.*, pp. 33-34.
3. J. Mill, *History of British India*, ix, London, 1826-35, p. 13.
4. *Fifth Report, op. cit.*, p. ccxciv.
5. *Ibid.*, p. cc xcvii.
6. *Ibid.*

greatly influenced by the economic doctrines of the Physiocrats. On 22 January 1776 Francis placed a rival plan on the minutes of the Council. Like Voltaire he 'considered inheritance as the best evidence of individual ownership'[1] and in support of this he "evoked the authority of James Stewart, Blackstone, Adam Smith, Montesquieu and Mirabeau." He advocated a fixed settlement with the zamindars whom he considered to be the lawful owner of the soil.[2] He recommended a perpetual settlement of the land revenue as calculated to promote the prosperity of the people. "The Jumma (assessment) once fixed, must be a matter of public record. It must be permanent and unalterable; and the people must, if possible, be convinced that it is so."[3] He made no concrete proposals for the protection of raiyats. A believer in the doctrine of laissez faire, then fashionable, he observed that if the Zamindars and raiyats "are left to themselves, they will come to an agreement in which each party will find advantage. The pottah is the evidence and security of this voluntary agreement."[4]

The Court of Directors, however, did not give their approval to any plan. "Having considered the different circumstances of letting your lands on leases for lives, or in perpetuity", the Court observed, "we do not for many weighty reasons think it at present advisable to adopt either of these modes."[5] Apparently the directors were in a state of indecision, and they had perhaps no solution of their own to offer. Instead of suggesting any sound principle of assessment, they therefore adhered to a temporary mode of annual settlement without public auction. They clearly pointed out that the lands should "in the meanwhile" be let "for succeeding year on the most advantageous terms," but not by public auction which they regarded as prejudicial to the interest of hereditary Zamindars. In 1778 they advised the repetition of the same mode.[6]

1. Ranjit Guha, *A Rule of Property for Bengal*, pp. 100-101.
2. *Fifth Report, op. cit.* p. xcix.
3. *Ibid.*, pp. ccc-cccxiii.
4. *Ibid.*, p. cciv.
5. Despatches to Bengal 24, December, 1776. para, 41 cited in B. B. Mishra, *op. cit.*, p. 183.
6. *Ibid.*

This prohibition of settlement by farming to the highest bidders represented a distinct gain to the Zamindars. On the termination of the quinquennial settlement in April 1777, the farmers were generally recalled, and the management of zamindaris was restored to their respective proprietors wherever they consented to hold them annually on the assessment of the previous year.[1] In 1781 Hastings established a Committee of Revenue[2] to "improve the figures of collection, which had reached by that time their lowest point since the Company's accession to the diwani."[3] This Committee no doubt showed an immediate improvement in collection when compared with the low return of 1780-81. But it did not attain the standard reached in the time of the Collectors between 1772 and 1774. The net revenue collected in 1780-81 amounted to 19,643,326 rupees. In 1781-82, it rose to 21,804,481. But it soon showed a decline and reached 20,318,167 rupees in 1783-84. The net figures of collection for 1772-73 and 1773-74 were 22,781,054 and 23,322,901 respectively.[4]

All the great zamindars of Bengal, all the ancient landed families, suffered under this system of annual settlements, frequent enhancements, and harsh methods of realisation. Old Zamindars, if they failed to compete with auction bidders, were turned out from estates which their forefathers had held for generations. If they kept their estates as farmers at an enhanced revenue and failed in prompt payment, on their estates were forced, managers who plundered the tillers of the soil and caused misery and depopulation.

Hasting's failure to restore collection to its former level brought discredit to his Government and put the Company in great financial distress which was aggravated in 1781 because of the combined threats of the Marathas, Mysore and France to the Company in India. On the top of all that, came unhappy developments at Benaras, where Hasting's own conduct was for the most part responsible for driving Chait Singh into rebellion. It caused a general disaffection of the people

1. *Ibid.*
2. *Fifth Report*, *op. cit.*, p. cccxxix.
3. B. B. Misra, p. 184.
4. Bengal Revenue Consultations, May 10, 1785, I. O. Range, 50, V. 58 f. 308, quoted in B. B. Misra, *op. cit.*, p. 184.

in Bihar, where most of the Zamindars used this opportunity to raise their standards of revolt against the English.[1] Although the revolt was put down and the war with the country powers won the financial crisis, which followed, in their wake, drove Government to the verge of bankruptcy.

These events greatly influenced the policy of the Company and the British Government. Pitt's India Act of 1784 ordered an enquiry into the complaints of the dispossessed Zamindars and directed the Company to take steps "for settling and establishing upon principles of moderation and justice, according to the laws and constitution of India, the permanent rules by which the tributes, rents and services of the Rajas, Zamindars, polygars, talukdars and other native landholders should be in future rendered and paid."[2]

In a letter of 22 December 1785 the Court of Directors pointed out that they wanted "to arrange a final system" for transacting business with the zamindars and other landlords.[3] That system they outlined in their letter of 12 April 1786, according to which the most likely means of avoiding defalcations would be to introduce a permanent settlement of the land revenue, estimate on reasonable principles, for the due payment of which the hereditary tenure of the possessor would be the best and the only necessary security.[4] They directed that the settlement should be made in all practicable instances with the zamindars, and they declared that "a moderate jumma or assessment, regularly and punctually collected, unites the consideration of our interests with the happiness of the natives and security of the landholders more rationally than any imperfect collection of any exaggerated jumma, to be enforced with severity and exaction."[5] And while they intended the settlement to be ultimately made permanent, they desired that the first settlement should be concluded for a period of ten years. After the conclusion of the decennial settlement, all the papers were to be sent to the Directors to enable them to form "a

1. J. Reginald Hand, *Early English Administration of Bihar*, 1781-85, Calcutta, 1897, pp. 4-24.

2. A. C. Guha, *op. cit.*, p. 77.

3. B. B. Misra, *op. cit.*, p. 185.

4. *Fifth Report*, *op. cit.*, p. 20.

5. *Ibid.*, p. 31.

conclusive and satisfactory opinion, so as to preclude the necessity of further reference or future change."[1]

Cornwallis deferred the conclusion of the decennial settlement till 1789 for further enquiry into the Bengal land system. During the years 1787 and 1788 annual settlements of revenue were made by Collectors, who were at the same time engaged in investigations prescribed by the Governor General.[2] The result of these enquiries are embodied in Shore's minutes of 1788 and 1789. Shore advocated that a permanent settlement with the zamindars would be beneficial for the country, but he thought it advisable to wait the result of further enquiry before making the system permanent.[3] Shore urged that the relations between the zamindars and the raiyats should be defined and adjusted, and rules for the enhancement of rent laid down before the Government demand was limited for ever.[4] Cornwallis recognised the value of such an enquiry but shrank from the delay which it involved. He believed that the effects of the limitation of public demand and the permanent settlement with the zamindars, combined with the regulations which he made for the grant of *pattas*, would place the relations between the zamindars and the raiyats on a proper footing.[5] The result of the enquiries was reported to the authorities in England in 1790. The Court of Directors deliberated over it for two years and gave their opinion in favour of a Permanent Settlement in their despatch of 19 September 1792.[6] This was the basis of the Proclamation of 22 March 1793 declaring the settlement to be permanent.

Political and administrative considerations no doubt were the major factors in the formulation of the land and revenue policies as contained in the Proclamation but these policies reflected familiarity with the principles of the classical political economy which were being developed in contemporary

1. A. C. Guha, *op. cit.*, p. 78.
2. *Fifth Report*, *op. cit.*, p. 21.
3. A. C. Guha, *op. cit.*, p. 84.
4. *Ibid.*
5. *Ibid.*, p. 86.
6. J. H. Harrington, [*An Elementary Analysis of the Laws and Regulations enacted by the Governor-General in Council at Fort William*,] iii, Calcutta, 1805-22, p. 359.

England and France. Indeed, the origins of the Permanent Settlement may be located "in that confluence of ideas where the two mainstreams of English and French thought merged in the second half of the eighteenth century."[1]

1. Ranjit Guha, *op. cit.*, preface

V

HISTORY OF LAND REVENUE IN CHOTANAGPUR
(c. 1770-1830 A.D.)

J. C. Jha

The land revenue system of the hilly and jungly tribal area of Jharkhand, called Chotanagpur division since 1854, has a peculiar interest for us; it provides a clear instance of the survival of the oldest land revenue system of India founded and consolidated by the Dravidians.[1] The plateau, which rises from some eight or ten hundred feet in the south-east to the height of three thousand six hundred feet in the west with well-cultivated plains on each terrace and the borders of each scarped and forest-clad,[2] had never been effectively subjugated before the British came to this area. Naturally enough, the tribal people could preserve their ancient land system. But during the Mughal period when the imperial authority established some contact with this area, the tribal chiefs were accepted as zamindars, and some of them got *sanads* on agreeing to pay a 'peshkash' or tribute.[3]

As the power of the East India Company was extended in the late eighteenth century the first contacts were made with the tribal chiefs. The grant of Mirkasim of 1760 gave the Company the territories later known as the Jungle Mahals and Dhalbhum in the Midnapur district; and the grant of the Diwani of 1765, besides confirming the former grant, added to the Company's territories the Chotanagpur estate with its dependent *parganas*, together with the other tribal areas such as, Palamau, Pachet, etc. But the real British penetration of the Jungle Mahals began in 1767,[4] and of Chotanagpur proper in 1769.[5]

1. Radha Kamal Mukerjee, *Land problems of India*, London, 1933, p. 34.
2. Baden-Powell, *The Land System of British India*, Oxford, 1892, p. 574.
3. According to the *Ain-i-Akbari*, (H. Blochmann, Ain-i-Akbari, Vol. I, Calcutta, 1872) this tributary area was known as Khukhra.
4. J. C. Jha, "Early British penetration into the Jungle Mahals," *JOBRS*, xlvi, parts I-IV.
5. J. C. Jha, "Early British penetration into Chotanagpur," *JBORS*, xliii, parts III & IV.

It was with great difficulty that the tribal chiefs were compelled to pay a fixed revenue to the Company. Only after a protracted military operation Jagannath Dhal of Dhalbhum agreed in 1777 to pay to the Company Rs. 2,000 for the first year, Rs. 3,000 for the second year and Rs. 4,000 for the third,[6] and this settlement was continued under the Decennial Settlement.[7] Finally, in 1800 it was raised to Rs. 4,267[8]. The *mahals* were now known as *hazuri* (paying revenue direct to the Government). By and large, the tribal chiefs were treated as zamindars of Grant's second class, i. e., made tributary by conquest, treaty or convention, without either full political or proprietary rights and yet not mere revenue collectors. Consequently, the tribal chiefs, who were also hinduised, changed their attitude towards the tribal peasantry.

In short, the British recognized the surviving rajas, chiefs and grantees as zamindars. Gradually the new revenue system was imposed by the Company, least realising that these tribal tillers of land had no experience of the survey and detailed assessment of the Mughals. The attempt to introduce a formal revenue system was likely to be ill received, and one which ignored tribal custom and feeling and which was operated by outsiders was certain to cause trouble.

In 1789 it was pointed out that the Permanent Settlement should not be extended to these tribal areas because the amount received from these *parganas* were "more in the nature of a tribute than a revenue proportioned to the produce of the soil.[9]" Yet the regulations of Cornwallis were applied to them, and "by the operation of selling estates for revenue balance", many of the zamindars were dispossessed.[10] As Hunter puts it, the Permanent Settlement "tried to suddenly substitute contract for custom."[11] The landlords now got unlimited powers of

6. L.S.S. O'Malley, *District Gazetteer, Singhbhum*, Saraikela & Kharsawan, Calcutta, 1910, p. 180.

7. Bengal Revenue consultation 19 of 27 March 1794 (53-14).

8. *D. G. Singhbhum*, p. 180.

9. L.S.S. O'Malley, *D. G. Manbhum*, 193, Calcutta, 1911.

10. Firminger, *Fifth Report*, vide O'Malley, *D. G. Midnapore*, 196, Calcutta, 1911. Raja of Pachet, Zamindar of Raipur and many others were even humiliated.

11. W. W. Hunter, *Bengal MS. Records* (1782-1807), i, London, 1894, p. 89.

increasing the rents of the cultivators; rackrenting ruined many families.

An important class of landholders affected by the new laws was that of the *ghatwāls* or *paiks* in the Jungle Mahals. The local leaders of the Bhumijes were the *sardar ghatwāls* (marcher lords), who, like the *mankis* of Chotanagpur proper and the *manjhis* of Santhal Parganas, had organised the tribal occupation and clearance of the lands. They were the circle heads guarding the passes and occupying a *taraf* (*jagir*) at a nominal rent as reward for their services, and maintained a permanent body of retainers—the *digwārs*, *ghatwāls* or village heads such as the *mundas* and *mahtos* of other areas, *sadials* and *tabedārs*,[12] enjoying different categories of lands. Under clause 4, section 8, Regulation I of 1793 the *ghatwāli* (*paikan*) lands were resumed, and the *ghatwāls* of Jungle Mahals were now required to pay Rs. 50,138 instead of Rs. 27,553.[13] A petition from the *ghatwāls* of Bishnupur sent to the Judge of Burdwan in May 1798 said : "We with our brethren have for many generations held the office of Ghautwals and Chowkedars. We have an allowance of lands and the sardars hold from 20 to 40 Begas at the most and our brethren under us hold from 5 to 14 Begas.."[14] But now suddenly they took to violence : the *heristadars*, *tahsildars*, the *darogas* and *barkandazas* were attacked at various places, and the whole area was in chaos and confusion.

At last the blunder committed by the Government was realised, and in 1799 these *jāgirs* were restored to the *ghatwāls*. The zamindars got back their police powers and the *ghatwāls* again became a part of the *zamindari* police. This *zamindari* or *ghatwāli* police system connected with the land grants has been a unique feature of this area. In 1805 it was extended to Pachet, Bagmundi, Bagankodar, Taraf Baleapar Kartas,

12. Tabedar, like *Chaukidar* or *gorait* in Chotanagpur proper, was on the lowest rung of the ladder. *Sadiala, ghatwāls* and *digwars* were almost synonymous : J. M. magistrate to Govt., 15 May 1832, para 4, B. C. 1501/58887

13. Board to Govt., 8 March 1799, Bang. Rev. Consultation, 32 of 15 March 1799 (54/1).

14. Petition, enclosure to Collector to Board, 4 May 1798, Guha and Mitra (ed.), *West Beng. Dist. Records, Burdwan*, 329, New series, Calcutta 1956.

Hasla, Jhalda, Jharia, Jaipur, Mukundpur, etc.[15] It was also recommended for the other areas of the Ramgarh district.

Indeed the existence of the *ghatwāli* lands was significant in as much as in these tenures not only was the chief entitled to his privileges, but "every head of a troop in his own grade and rank, and every militiaman had lesser share in the privilege."[16] According to Radha Kamal Mukerjee, "the outlying districts of a conquered territory, in the Dravidian scheme" were occupied by these *ghatwāl* chiefs like the *poligars* of south India.[17] This "system of tribal territories and subdivisions, through a system of military aids, investiture of the tribal chiefs and patriarch by the raja, and other feudal incidents" could be found among the Gonds in Madhya Pradesh and Berar, the Mundas and Oraons in Chotanagpur and the Kandhs in Orissa.[18] The raja or chief occupied the central territory and the *ghatwāls* the fringes. A. C. Guha thinks that there is "considerable variety" in the tenures known under the general name of *ghatwālī* in different parts of the country, but "they all agree in this that they are grants of land situated on the edge of the hilly country, and held on condition of guarding the ghats or passes."[19]

In the whole of the Chotanagpur plateau there were headmen of villages, their names varying from area to area. As among the Mundas of Chotanagpur proper, there was, among the Hos of Kolhan a *munda* as the head of every village. After the military operation of 1819-20 Major Roughsedge fixed a rent of eight annas per plough, and after the final annexation of this area in 1836-37 this system was confirmed by Wilkinson.[20] The *munda* of every village now became responsible for the collection of the land revenue to the British Government's representatives in the South-West Frontier

15. Bengal Cr. Judl. Consultation 16 of 13 Dec. 1805 (129/18).

16. Baden-Powell, *op. cit.*, 582.

17. Radha Kamal Mukerjee, *op. cit.*; 33.

18. *Ibid.* p. 32.

19. Guha and infra *op. cit.*, Appendix, 419: they are said to have existed in Birbhum, Bankura, Burdwan, Bhagalpur, Monghyr, Manbhum Purnea, Patna and the Santhal Parganas.

20. J. C. Jha, "British Occupation of Kolhan" 1836-37, *Proceedings I.H.C.*, 1965.

Agency. A *manki* was to supervise the works of the *mundas* of several villages. Both the *munda* and *manki* got some commission on the revenue collected.[21] He had some police duties too, and he settled an abandoned holding or uncultivated land.

The Mundas of Chotanagpur proper (modern Ranchi district) were probably the original clearers of the land. Originally they had no central authority like a raja, and their settlements were divided into parhas of 15 to 20 or even 25 villages, each under its *manki* and local *munda*.[22] The local chiefs probably received no rent, but only assistance in war and a *salāmī* at festivals. The *munda* was the head of the village, but the final authority rested with the *manki* or the *mankis* in council united with the *mundas*. This, according to Baden-Powell, "resembled the Dravidian form of South India where the village or other family groups were aggregated into unions called *nād* or *nādu* with some kind of chief, acting as regards the 'nad', or in council with other chief in affairs affecting the whole country".[23]

The Oraons of this area perhaps occupied lands already cleared by the Mundas. The main source of revenue of their chiefs was the special landholding in each village. The villages were divided into lots or '*khunts*', one of these being the *majhas* land or royal farm, another going to the headman, and yet another to the *pāhan* or priest for the worship of the great goddess, the district god, and the village deity.[24] Eventually the chief, called raja, not satisfied with the *majhas*, began to take a grain-share also from all lands except the priest's and the headman's. The *mahto* served as an accountant, getting his allotment of land. Such lands and those held by *bhuinhars* or original clearers, were exempt from tax. To provide for the cultivation of the royal farm or *majhas* land, the king made an allotment (*betkheta*) to certain cultivators, which was exempt from revenue on condition that they should work the *majhas* lands. Thus all lands except the lands of the *bhuinhars* and the

21. Radha Kamal Mukerjee, *op. cit.*, p. 32.

22. Davidson to Ouseley, 29 Aug. 1839, para 3, no. 247 Misc. Dispatch Book, G. G.'s Agent's office, Patna Archives.

23. Baden-Powell, *op. cit.*, p. 117. Also see R. K. Mukerjee., *op. cit.*, p. 33.

24. *Ibid.*, p. 119.

betkheta paid a share to the king or chief, and was called 'Rajhas' land.

In the early years of the Munda settlement, there seems to have been no individual ownership of land. The tribesmen cleared their village lands under the leadership of their headman or *munda* and village priest or *pāhan*, who were responsible for re-allocating lands and collecting such dues or services as were owed to the community. No regular system of revenue seems to have existed. But the *munda* and the *ıanki* held lands in their respective jurisdictions and perhaps gifts of grain were received.[25] The unoccupied land belonged to the *parha*, and gradually all the waste lands were occupied.

The Cheros and Kharwars of Palamau had a number of *jagirdars* during this period. Raja Gopal Rai, the chief of Palamau, had agreed to pay Rs. 12,000 revenue a year to the East India Company in 1771.[26] He, however, became a tool in the hands of Udwant Ram Quanungo. The destruction of the raja's estate thus begun was completed by the Decennial Settlement. Certain old *jagirdars* were allowed to pav their revenue through the raja, but many new men were confirmed as *jagirdars,* even though they had acquired them in a doubtful way. The result was a fall in the income of the raja and in his prestige *vis-a-vis* his *jagirdars*. Subsequently the raja's estate was sold up for arrears of revenue, and the *jagirdars* remained a constant source of trouble.

In such *parganas* of Chotanagpur proper, as Tamar, Rahi and Baranda, which were difficult of approach and strongly fortified by nature, something of this village organisation survived even into the nineteenth century. S. T. Cuthbert, the Ramgarh magistrate, described the way the headmen and village priests transacted the village business, calling the villagers together in May and distributing to those wishing to cultivate their different portions of land.[27] No *patta* or written document was given; the extent of the cultivator's *jote* or field was shown before witnesses, and a piece of earth as a token of acceptance was taken from the headmen or *mahto* as he was called in some areas.

25. *Ibid.*, 117.
26. J. C. Jha, *The Kol Insurrection in Chotanagpur,* Calcutta, 1964, p. 9.
27. S. T. Cutchbert to Govt., 1 April 1827, para 36, Beng. Cr. Judl. Consultation, of 14 June 1827. (158/22)

Above the village was a wider tribal division, the *parha* or *patti* under a circle headman called the *manki*. The *mankis* had much influence over the tribal masses and at festival times, when the members of the *parha* assembled "to hunt, amuse themselves and decide disputes" the *mankis* exercised considerable authority.[28] Each *parha* had its distinguishing flag, "the attempt to make use of which by the Coles of another purha at their festivals immediately leads to serious quarrels."[29] John Davidson, the Assistant political agent at Lohardagga, saw this system in parts of *parganas* Khukhra and Sonepur in 1839.

Tribal society was already feeling the unhappy effects of the hinduisation of the tribal chiefs of the area when the British brought in their complex, legalistic revenue system to it. Both impacts introduced foreign notions and foreign people into the area, leading to the ruin of the tribal peasantry. Neither these hinduised chiefs nor the English administrators, born and bred in the tradition of agricultural landlordism, had any sympathy with the tradition of tribal ownership of land. The non-tribal settlers and subordinate officers took advantage of the British laws/and exploited the peasants.

Thus in the first half of the nineteenth century the traditional tribal society was being undermined: custom was being undermined by contract, a barter economy by a money economy they had not yet learnt to handle, and divisions of the land determined by tribal custom were replaced bv a landlordtenant relationship.

The new non-tribal *diwans*, *tahsildars*, priests and others got extensive grants of land. Some of the newcomers, Baraiks, Rajputs and Rauteas, even held *jagir* at fixed rents which were granted for the performance, as Davidson reported, of military services—services used to cow down the tribal subjects.[30] The brahmans secured equally extensive grants of land, especially in the Khukhra and Doesa *parganas*. Davidson in 1839 described the brahmans and individuals of other castes, who had come from below the ghauts and enjoy grants of land generally by their purchase at fixed rents from the different Rajas, some-

28. Davidson to Ouseley, 29 Aug. 1829, para 3, no. 247, Misc. Despatch Book, G. G.'s Agent's Office. Patna Archives.

29. *Ibid.* para 3.

30. *Ibid.*, para. 6.

times also rent-free, and also grants of rent-free lands for religious purposes, in the mode usually given by Hindoos.[31] Needless to say, all these outsiders—including even Muslim merchants and servants of the maharaja and dependent rajas—were provided with land at the expense of the tribal cultivators.

Here and there, it is true, local conditions enabled the *mankis* and *mundas* to survive, and to protect tribal landholdings, as in remote Tamar and Sonepur, where the original heads of villages were strong enough to inspire fear. Elsewhere, however, the headmen "were entirely dispossessed and replaced Suds (foreigners) or their villagers (were) resumed by the Raja himself."[32]

The East India Company raised the amount of tribute payable by the Maharaja of Chotanagpur in stages : the tribute fixed for him in 1771 was Rs. 4,000; in 1774 it was raised to Rs. 15,001; and under the Permanent Settlement (Regulation I of 1793) it became Rs. 15,043-9.[33] This naturally led to rack-renting; the tribal peasantry was taxed more and more. The maharaja had undertaken not to exact from the *raiyats* any cesses, except the customary ones, and not to take *mangan* and exact *begar*. Nonetheless he imposed heavy burdens of his own upon the people; even though he received about Rs. 338,077 from his *jagirdars* and further amounts from Tori *pargana* and from a number of *bhandar* villages (lands of which were under his direct possession and cultivation), he also imposed a number of *abwabs* or cesses.[34] Whenever he bestowed a *jagir* or confirmed a *sanad* to the heirs of a deceased *jagirdar* he expected a *nazarana* of 1,000 to 1,500 rupees. Several gifts and contributions (*madad*, *māngan*, etc.) were exacted.

The chiefs, *jagirdars* and other superior tenure-holders had no right under tribal custom to increase the rent of the village lands, nor could they drive out the old cultivators. But these age-old customs were now frequently violated by the non-tribal farmers in the early years of the nineteenth century.

31. *Ibid.*, para. 10.

32. *Ibid.*, para. 8.

33. J. Reid. *Ranchi Settlement Report* (1902-1910), Calcutta, 1912, para 34.

34. Cuthbert to Govt., 21 April 1827, para. 11, Beng. Cr.. Judl. Consultation 53 of 14 June 1827 (132/22). About Rs. 80,000 came from the *bhandar* villages annually.

Again, where the rent had been paid in service—three days ploughing, three days' work with the spade, three days of ric-planting and three days of harvest work and so on—the new owners came to demand far more work than custom had permitted.[35] *Thikadars* or revenue farmers came to cultivate considerable areas by forced labour exacted without limit from the tribal ryots.

The *bhuinhars* (the original clearers of the land, e.g., the *munda* and the *manki*) had a hereditary interest in the land, and even when they fled the village, they had a right to reclaim the land on their return. But now the non-tribal farmers not only refused to recognise the right of their heirs, but also took possession of the land on their leaving the village. Not only that, but by harassing them in the courts or in the police *thanas*, they forced the *bhuinhars* to leave the village.[36]

Thus the first half of the nineteenth century saw great changes in the land revenue system of this tribal area. Unfortunately when the local chiefs were unsympathetic towards the peasant's cause no sympathetic British revenue officer was deputed to this area before Wilkinson became the Political Agent. Naturally enough, severe exactions by the non-tribal farmers of revenue, and the grant of a large number of tribal landholdings to oppressive foreigners led to recurrent unrest from 1792 to 1832.

35. Davidson to Cuseley, 29 August 1839, para. 14, no. 247, Misc. Despatch Book, G. G's Agents Office, Patna Archives.

36. *Ibid.*, para. 19.

VI

THE MUNDA LAND SYSTEM AND REVENUE REFORMS IN CHOTANAGPUR DURING 1869-1908

Suresh Singh

The forty years from the passage of the Chotanagpur Tenure Act (1869) to that of the Chotanagpur Tenancy Act (1908) constitute a formative period in the history of Chotanagpur. It witnessed the complete disintegration of tribal agrarian system and experiments in the formulation of land revenue policy towards tribal people. This period coincided with the Sardars' legal and constitutional agitation and with Birsa's political and religious movement. Out of these long years of turmoil emerged the present land revenue administration in Chotanagpur.

Tribal agrarian system : nature and disintegration

There developed two theories about the nature of the tribal agrarian system in the heart of Chotanagpur, The early British administrators, S. T. Cuthbert, John Davidson and E. T. Dalton built up the theory of tribal peasant proprietorship; the *bhuinhars* or original clearers of the lands held their lands rent-free or at half the village rent, and they were later reduced to the status of the ordinary *raiyats*[1] by aliens. This theory was reiterated by the German missionaries with their German agrarian background[2] and by their Sardar wards, who clamoured for the restoration of their rights to the *bhuinhars* or peasant proprietors. During the *bhuinhari* settlement of 1869-1880, Rakhal Das Haldar, Special Commissioner, in the course of his investigation into land revenue system, stumbled upon new facts and characterised the tribal agrarian system or *khunt-katti* system in Chotanagpur as a "non-Aryan commune."[3]

1. See *Papers relating to Chotanagpur Agrarian Disputes* (*PAC* pp. 1-6).
2. J. Reid, *Final report on survey and settlement operations in the Districts of Ranchi*, 1902-10, Calcutta, 1912, p. 86 (quoted).
3. *Infra*, footnote 21.

Haldar only took notice of the communal system; he did not develop any theory about it. Only after the Birsa movement, which started in *khuntkatti* region, and the consequent preparation of Rev. J. Hoffmann's famous memorandum on the *khuntkatti* system,[4] followed by the able studies of Sarat Chandra Roy,[5] the "communal" character of the Mundas' agrarian system could be fully recognised. Both Hoffmann and Roy were at pains to prove that agrarian disorders in Chotanagpur resulted from the disintegration of the original communal order into non-communal, feudal or Zamindari systems.[6] But this significant finding was not based on any detailed and scientific investigation. Both Roy and Hoffmann attributed the dilution and disintegration of the communal system to the influence of the *dikus*, the aliens. Except for some hints, they did not clearly indicate the range of acculturation, the extent to which non-tribal communities had been absorbed into their agrarian system and contributed to its present character. They also oversimplified the historical process of disintegration of the communal system. Roy overlooked the inner contradictions in the tribal body politic, the antagonism between Mundas and Pāhans, sharpened by the British contact with them.[7]

Tribal agrarian system in Chotanagpur was shaped by the interplay of Kolarian Munda, Bhumij and Dravidian (Oraons, Kharias and Nagas or Naghansis) agrarian elements. The Dravidian elements[8] were : institution of kingship (Raja) with special powers, division of villages into *khunts*, rent-free tenures for worship of gods and for village chiefs, creation of *rajhus* tenure for Raja and his "grain-share" etc. The Kolarian system, probably communal (Munda agrarian system today has more communal elements than Oraon) did not provide for kingship and central government and was without any regular system of payment of revenue. As a result of the inter-

4. Rev. J. Hoffmann, *Encyclopaedia Mundarica*, s. v. "*Khuntkatti*", iii, Calcutta, 1912, pp. 2402-2404.

5. S. C. Roy, *Mundas and their Country*; See Roy's article "The Administrative history and land tenures of the Ranchi district under British Rules, *Man In India*, [illegible], pp. 276-323.

6. *Ibid.*

7. *Ibid.*

8. B. H. Baden-Powell, *The Land Systems British India*, Oxford, 1892, pp. 118-120.

mixture of the two racial systems the Dravidian (Naga) institution of kingship was grafted on to the Munda institutions. *Patti*, and such special tenures (as names will indicate) as *deotar mahtoi*, *majhias* were incorporated into the agrarian complex that developed in Chotanagpur. The important tribal communities, such as Mundas Bhumij and Oraons developed from pastoral into agricultural communities. The Nagas (later *Nagbansi* Rajputs) spearheaded the process of the hinduisation of tribes in Chotanagpur, introduced new techniques of production including improved implements (*nayal* plough) and concept of agricultural seasons (*nakshatra*) and days and months and thus contributed to the process of the transformation of these tribes.

The basis of the tribal (Munda) social order was the totemic clan system.[9] The tribe was divided into *kili* (clan) which was subdivided into families which formed the unit of production. It was something of an odd "non-Aryan commune"[10] adapted to the institutions of the patriarchal family. Elements of communal life were shared by the members of or the descendants from the male line of the original founders of the village. The principle that those who reclaimed the land owned it or that proprietory right grew out of one's "creative or formative work"[11] was the basis of the agrarian order. Thus, a Munda would say : "we cut the forest, we plough and sow and weed and properly reap, and Singbonga (Supreme God) sends the rain and the sunshine. What have they—the *dikus*—done ?"[12] The daughters had (and still have) no

9. Hoffmann repudiates the totemic basis of the Munda order ("Kili", *Encyclopaedia Mundarica*, viii, p. 2413). This cannot be accepted as some of the septs or clans are unmistakably totemic.

10. Rakhal Das Haldar, "An account of the village system of Chotanagpur", Appendix to Resolution by the Government of Bengal, Rev. Depptt., 25 Nov. 1880. *Papers Relating to Chotanagpur Agrarian Disputes*, i, p. 102, D.L.R.

11. Rev. J. Hoffmann, "Principles of succession and Inheritance among the Mundas", *Man In India*, xlli, pp. 324-38.

12. *Ibid.* Thus the Mundas would not recognise any intermediary interest. The Raja, later a political necessity or unwarranted "graft on their system" and the hordes of middlemen who poured in, could in their imagination acquire no right to their land. Quit-rent per village quite independent of the area under cultivation as prevalent in the *khuntkatti* village was "the racial law". The Raja did not claim anything beyond the quit-rent and certainly not the proprietory right to Munda village.

right to property because only those who worked on and created the landed property shared it. The lands within the village were owned not by an individual but by the members of the family founded by the original settler. No individual of the village could alienate the family or communal lands like *sarna* (the sacrificial grove), *sasan* (the burial ground), pastures, forest etc. They did not pay rent but voluntary subscription (called *chanda*) to their overlord or the Raja. who did not claim in theory or in practice any proprietory right over their lands. There were *raiyats*, low Hindu caste relatives on the female side of the *khuntkattidars* such as Swansi, Ghasis, Bhogtas or Mahilis, Khangars (not called *dikus* but accepted by the Munda as indispensable adjuncts of their society) performing non-agricultural functions necessary to the village life. These were subordinate to the main family in the village. The family was fortified by religious ties, institutions of ancestor worship festivals and by social occasions, and had its own moral code rigorously enforced under a patriarchal authority. The community consisting of the large number of families, descendants of common ancestors, looked upon itself as a unit and appointed *pāhan* to perform religious functions. He was the oldest or eldest member of the family of the original founder and the head of the village family. He presided over Panchayat called to settle various kinds of disputes, inflicted punishment, collected and transmitted the *chanda*, and served as the custodian of tradition and customs. The Munda was only second in rank to the *pāhan* and his assistant.[13] In some

13. A somewhat different account of what was the original relationship between the *pāhan* and the Mundas has been given by R. D. Haldar (see the above-mentioned account), "What the Manki was to the Parha, the Munda was to the village; but he was something more. He was the head of secular affairs, and at the same time a joint proprietor of the village with the *pāhan* and in some cases with the Mahto also. Somewhat subordinate to the Mundas in secular affairs, he was master of the invisible world, and no less a proprietor of the village than the Munda. If the Munda was charged with guarding against human foes, it was the *pāhan's* special business to propitiate the invisible spirits for protecting village from blights, droughts, diseases and other calamities. He held certain lands in the village by virtue of his office. The *pāhan* was by no means a mere village priest as we find him in many places in these days." Of the two accounts, Hoffmann's is more plausible as the totemic character of the clan and social system and the mode of sacrifices to spirits etc. might have imparted a relative significance to the *pāhan's* office.

villages the two offices were combined in the same family. The manifestation of "consciousness of a belonging together, of the family tie"[14] on a higher level was (and still is) the institution of Mankiship, the secular head of a *pati.* The families are grouped into villages, ten or more of such villages belonging to the same sept. The *manki* was the "great referee on points of social disputes",[15] or those relating to land and property and other family matters; his duty was also to represent the family, in its dealing with the Maharaja, to defend the interests of any of his villages against attempts or aggressions of any kind from another sept or family.

The larger institutions of *parha* and *patti* are historically interesting: these are more geographical than social. The original institution was *patti,* as it survives to this day in the closed *khuntkatti* regions; the *parhas* (which are hinduised and the Parha Maharaja of Koerara has today assumed the paraphernalia of extinct Hindu zamindars) exist in the "exposed" Bhuinhari region. Moreover, *parhas* are socially homogeneous; in Bhuinhari area villages of some *kili* or clan cluster together. *Pattis* are more heterogeneous; their villages are inhabited by people of many classes, because of the historical reason of their being founded by settlers from the Tamar and Nagari regions, who were expelled by the *dikus,* in the wake of uprisings.

The interplay of Dravidian and Kolarian elements introduced many features in the Munda agrarian system : the special tenure for Raja, *rajhas* ; that for village deities, *bhutkheta*; for village sacrificer, *pahnai,* and for his assistant, *panbhara*; for village head man, *mahtoi.* The original Munda land system was therefore diluted: the *bhuinhari* could be regarded as only a "decaying" form of *khuntkatti* : the *bhuinhari* underlined individual proprietorship, and the *khuntkatti* family proprietorship. During the latter half of the 19th century the communal system disintegrated apace. Several factors contributed to the process. The practice of the Raja of granting *kharposh* (maintenance *jagirs*) of tribal villages to his multiplying relations and that of the latter of granting similar *kharposh* to

14. Hoffmann, "Principles of succession and Inheritance among the Mundas" *op. cit.,* p. 335.

15. R. D. Haldar, "An account of the village system of Chotanagpur," *op. cit.,* p. 102.

their relations set in motion a chain-reaction of forces that undermined the tribal agrarian system in Lodhma, Govindpur, Kokariah in Ranchi District.[16]

There was also an influx of Brahmins and Rajputs, merchants and businessmen, military adventures and money-lenders from outside. Rautias, a semi-martial people, came from Berar, and Rajputs and Brahmins from the north. Service *jagirs* were granted to them.[17] This process must have started much earlier than the year 1676, the year of probably the first grant of *patta*. During medieval times, the Muslims and other communities followed in the wake of the Mughal armies into Chotanagpur. Raja Durjan Sal brought artisans and masons and Rautias, who later constituted the militia of the king. The Kurmis expelled the Kols from the western part of Manbhum district[18] and obtained a footing among the aboriginal tribes, and gradually in more than one part of Manbhum supplanted them.[19] In Manbhum the system was broken up under pressure from the local rajas, and the *khuntkattidars* were reduced to the status of the *mukarraridars*. The Mundas were further driven out of the fertile lands of Panchpargana into the hills and fastnesses of southern Khunti, Tamar and Bundu police stations. With the coming of the British in 1785 an element of stability was slowly introduced, and the pace of the influx of the aliens and the disintegration of the system quickened. The construction of the Grand Trunk Road, cutting its way through the jungles of Manbhum and Hazaribagh, opened up the wildest district "to the civilising influence of traders, the keen-eyed Hindu merchants."[20] With the

16. See Haldar, "An Account of the village system in Chotanagpur" PAC, p 104.

17. *Ibid.*

18. S. C. Roy, *The Mundas and their country*, p. 145.

19. E. T. Dalton, *Descriptive Ethnology of Bengal*, Calcutta, 1872, p. 306. "There were traditions of struggles between them and the Kolarian aborigines of these regions and though the latter generally managed to hold their own, in some place Kurmi villages (were) established on sites which we know from the groups (318) of rude stone pillars or cenotaphs still conspicuous were once occupied by Bhumij or Munda, and in others vestings in ruined temples appertaining to successive generations of Kurmis amidst village that have for ages been occupied by Bhumij".

20. F. B. Bradley Birt, *Chotanagpur, a little known province of the Empire*, London, 1919, pp. 5-6.

construction of the railways timber gained a sudden market value.[21] The land hunger in the 18th and 19th century in north Bihar and Bengal might have accelerated the pace of the influx. Thus, though the seeds of agrarian trouble had been sown before the establishment of British dominion, it was during the years 1806 and 1895, "the most fatal ones for the Mundas in particular and the aboriginals in general",[22] that the spoliation of the agrarian system on a wide scale took place.

A distinction has, however, to be made between the *jagirdars* who had lived among the Mundas for centuries and those who appeared in the first or second decade of the nineteenth century. The former, the "predecessors of the Nagvansi Rajputs, Rautia and Bhiwan *illaquadars*"[23] had "lived among the *Kols* for many generation past" so much so that in many matters their interests were identical with theirs, and those of them who were not 'utterly devoid of common sense or common humanity could scarcely fail to see the great usefulness of the aboriginal cultivators. Thus, "a considerable portion of the old *jagirdars* lived peaceably with their tenants." True, some of them suppressed them but could have "hardly done more in oppressing the tenantry than would have been done by even better educated *zamindars* under similar circumstances." Though the old *jagirdars* had wrecked the Mundari *khuntkatti* system over a part of the Munda land, their oppression had been by and large "borne with"[24] partly for the reason that the Mundas had still some lands left in the hilly areas of southern Khunti and western Tamar to fall back upon.

The new class of *jagirdars* coming up towards the end of the eighteenth and the beginning of the nineteenth century were of a different kind[25] and a "far worse class of men."[26] The year 1822 when Maharaja Jagarnath Sahi Deo ascended his ancestral gadi was *annus terribilis* because it coincided with letting loose into the country infamous *thikadars*, Hindus,

21. *Ibid.*, p. 7.

22. Hoffmann, *Encyclopaedia Mundarica*, ii, s. v., pp. 512-13.

23. Babu R. D. Haldar to D. C. Lohardaga, No. 11, Ranchi, 22 May 1880, *P.A.C.*, i, p. 83.

24. *Ibid.*

25. Hoffmann, *Encyclopaedia Mundarica*, ii, s.v. "*Bhuinhari*", *ibid.*, vol. ii, pp. 517-18.

26. Haldar to D. C., 22nd May 1880, op. cit.

Musalmans and Sikhs and some others who originally came "as horse dealers and shawl and brocade merchants, and obtained farms of villages instead of cash, of which latter the chiefs were always in want". The process of the influx in the plains of Panchpargana had started towards the end of the eighteenth century. The aliens in Panchpargana[27] were mostly peasants (Kurmis) from neighbouring areas, while those in Sonepur or the heart of the Munda area were merchants and *thikadars*, who, having a "temporary interest in the villages", tried to squeeze" as much as abwabs as possible from the ryots in shape of rents, *swabs* and Salamis".[28] It was this class, the hated *dikus*, that was to bring about the total disintegration of the tribal land system in the 19th century.

The jagirdars or *thikadars* were granted *jagirs* or temporary leases of villages not only in consideration of military services or those of a "civil or religious nature" but also "at the pleasure of the superior"[29] proprietor. They were better equipped and organised than the Mundas. They gradually demanded payments of various kinds, and greatly increased services. In 1856 the number of *jagirdars* stood at about 600, and they held from "a portion of a village to 150 villages."[30] By 1874, the Deputy Commissioner, Ranchi, reported that the "authority of the old Munda or Uraon chiefs" had been "almost entirely effaced by that of Hindu farmers, introduced by the superior landlord or by the numerous holders of religious or maintenance grants". In some villages the aborigines had "completely lost their proprietory rights", and had been "reduced to the position of farm labourers". The *modus operandi* of the elements consisted of the use of force in expelling the owners of the plan, legal measures, imposition of rent, illegal enhancement, praedial conditions and forced labour.

In the first phase the *jagirdars* were foisted on Mundas and Mankis on the strength of the *pattas* issued by the Raja, and legal owners were evicted by brutal force. The persistent attempts to reduce the Mundas to the status of *raiyats* suc-

27. Panchpargana consists of the police stations of Silli, Sonahatu (Barenda and Rahe) Bundu and Tamar of the Ranchi District.

28. Haldar to D. C., *op. cit.*

29. S. T. Cuthbert to Secy. to Govt. of Bengal in the Judicial Deptt. Fortwilliam, 14 June 1827 (called Cuthbert's Report).

30. S. C. Roy, *the Mundas and their country*, p. 119.

ceeded on account of the ignorance of the courts of the tribal rights and customs. The landlords forcibly took possession of *bhuinhari* lands and included them in their *majhias* lands on the death of the *bhuinhars* or when they left their village or were induced to leave their homes.[31] Though force was the first and infallible weapon in the armoury of the newcomers, they did not fail to employ the legal means when it suited their purpose. They posed as zamindars and tried their best and with success to impose the Bengal concept of the *raiyat*-landlord relationship on the Mundas and establish it before the courts. In the civil suits or criminal cases instituted by these aliens against the Mankis and Mundas their documentary evidence naturally outweighed the oral evidence or unwritten traditions of the ignorant Mundas. The courts, ignorant of the incidence of the Mundari *khuntkatti* tenure, confused the Munda land system with the *zamindari* system.

As a corollary to the imposition of their status or proprietory rights as zamindars, the *dikus* sought to change the voluntary subscription or quit-rent interest, and incidence of zamindari system. Reid catalogues the following twenty-one praedial conditions or *rakumats* : *dasai* (payment to the landlord at the time of Dasahara), *batta* (an allowance for exchange of sicca rupees into Company's rupees), *bhatta* (a charge to meet the expenses of the landlord and his servants on their visit to village), *rashid likhai* (payment at the time of giving rent receipts), *dak mushara* (dak cess), *neg* (customary payment on marriage etc.), *nawarkhani* (a contribution of rice on an auspicious day), *dan pancha* (contribution made by a *raiyat* cultivating *tanr*), *ninako dhan, bhandari dhan* (contribution for support of village *bhandari*), *ogra dhan* (contribution for support of village official who guarded forest), *mahua beheri* (for enjoyment of *mahua*), *kathar beheri* (for jack fruit tree), *rakhi beheri* (for Rakhi festival), *brahmni niksari* (fee to Brahmin at various festivals), *shikar khasi* (presents to be given to zamindar when he went out for shooting), *thana kharcha* (for support of police), *dardan ghee* (ghee offered at the time of *dasai*), *saltmani* (cash payment at the end of agricultural operation), etc.[32]

31. Extract from a letter from Dr. John Davidson, Principal Asstt., Governor General's Agent, to Major J. R. Ouseley, G. G.'s Agent Kishenpore (No. 247, 28th August, 1839) *PAC*, i. p. 6.

32. Reid, *op. cit.*, pp. 87-89.

The incidence of forced labour (*beth begari*) renderable in a typical village in Ranchi was found to be as follows : 3 days' ploughing (*har*), 3 days' digging (*kori*), 3 days' planting or sowing (*ropini*), 3 days' cutting (*kotni*), 1 day's thrashing (*misri*), 1 day's storing the grain (*morabandhi*), 1 or 2 days' 'carrying to landlords' godown on his journeys (*des bides*)—in all 15 days.[33]

The machinations of the *dikus* led to the destruction of the tribal agrarian system in Tamar and Khunti regions.[34]

The influx of aliens and the introduction of the institutions and functionaries of British administration upset the traditional Munda society, reversed the relative positions of *pāhans* and *munda* respectively. Hitherto the *munda* was only the first assistant and right hand man of the *pāhan*. Now the two functionaries came into sharp conflict with each other. The animosity between the *munda* and the *pahan* led to the refusal by the second to pay any contribution to the first. Because of this internal strife both *munda* and *pāhan* failed to pay dues and so were sued for arrears by superior landlord, and their villages were sold up. Secondly,[35] the *munda*, who was first merely a *primus inter pares* in the community and nothing more than that, sought to arrogate more authority to himself like alien zamindars with disastrous consequences to the community. Sometimes the alien landlords sought to win over the *mundas* by granting lands to them and thus playing off one set of *mundas* against the other. The headman or *munda* posed as zamindar, "borrowed money from a local moneylender, executed a document in his favour", and pledged the whole village as security. The moneylender accepted the security. The *munda* being unable to pay the debt, the village was sold in auction as a zamindari village. The purchaser would enhance *chandas* or subscriptions by the *khuntkattidars* and treated them as rent. If a person refused to pay, the new landlord sued him for rent and got a decree. The broken *khuntkatti* villages bear a testimony to the rapacity of self-styled *munda* zamindars. These were the villages in which the

33. *Ibid.*, pp. 90-91.
34. *Ibid.*, pp. 81-84.
35. Hoffmann, *Encyclopaedia Mundarica*, viii, s. v. "*Khuntkatti*", p. 2399,

munda appropriated the rent of the *parias*, obtained the control of the jungle, enhanced the *chandas* payable by the other members or reduced the other members, with the exception of near relatives (*khorposhdars*) and the *pahans*, to the position of ordinary *raiyats*.[36]

The British system of justice contributed inadvertently to the breakdown of the agrarian system. Though "the impartiality of the European judges and officials" could not be questioned "in the remote degree", they laboured under "a great disadvantage in not understanding the language spoken by the majority of the inhabitants of this province, i.e. Mundari or Uraon". The court language, a mixture of Hindi and Urdu words, was a "prefect crux" to the people. This difficulty brought in the "court officials", such as pleaders, etc., who could "easily influence the decision" of the European officers by "false interpretation."[37] Justice was not only costly, it was also delayed. The parties had to wait for weeks and months, and during their absence from villages, the tax-farmers could "commit new depredations."[38] According to the "unanimous testimony of the Kolhs" the lodging of reports at the police station would involve payment of any amount from four *annas* to one rupee to the thana-writer in case of a death case ; sudden death would involve greater sums. Only the "less ignorant" and thus "more capable of holding their own against the police" could "get off without payment."[39]

Experiments in agrarian legislations :

Against the background of the disintegration of the agrarian system the authorities sought mainly to determine the rights of *raiyats*, define the privilege of landlords, regulate rent and praedial conditions and forced labour through either piecemeal legislations and proposed introduction of the Bengal Tenancy Act or through the Survey and Settlement operations.

The administrative measures following the Kol Insurrection did not touch the question of agrarian security for tribal peasantry, which was the core of the agrarian problem. The

36. *Ibid.*, pp. 2399-2400-1. Also see, Reid, *op. cit.*, p. 84.
37. From Revd. H. Onasch and 15 others to H. H. to Lt. Governor of Bengal, 17th May, 1876, *PAC*, i, p. 68.
38. *Ibid.*, p. 69.
39. *Ibid.*

middlemen, who were expelled, returned and avenged themselves on the tribes and contributed to the breakdown of the agrarian system.[40] Peasant proprietory tenure[41] suffered the greatest disturbance after the Kol insurrection and when many Kols left the country. The farmers and sub-proprietors objected to their re-entry when they returned after some years; both of them refused to return their lands which the Kols claimed. It was this class of uprooted *bhuinhars* that constituted the nucleus of the Sardar movement.

With the spread of Christianity among the Mundas the agrarian question took a new turn. The tribals' motive in joining the mission, except in a few cases, were not spiritual but purely secular. Major Hannygton, Deputy Commissioner, Ranchi, stressed during the visit of H. Ricketts in 1854-55 the necessity to "protect these under tenures", which was "essential to the permanent tranquillity of the country", with little subsequent effect. In 1859 the Commissioner proposed the introduction of Act I of 1859 in the Chotanagpur Division with some modification. The Board of Revenue objected to the extension of the distraint clauses of the Act for the benefit of the Lohardaga landowners[42] and felt that it could not be "safely" introduced. The existing procedure for disposal of revenue suit was modified in accordance with its spirit, and the Commissioner continued to hear appeals.

There was, however, a temporary reaction in favour of the Kols, and the establishment of the courts "for cheap and easy administration of justice led the Kols to believe that the Government was partial to them.[43] They had by this time learnt "successfully the tactics of their Hindu landlords", instituted a large number of cases for restoration of lands with varying results under the impression that Government "favoured their claims". The majority of these were "utterly false.[44] Armed with decree copies they forcibly took possession of

40. Haldar to D. C., Lohardagga, No. 11, Ranchi, 22 May 1860 *PAC*, i, p. 83.

41. Dalton, to Secy. to Govt. of Bengal (Rev.) No. 297, Camp Chaibasa, 23 December 1871, *ibid*, p. 121.

42. Reid, *op. cit.*, p. 33.

43. Haldar to D. C., Lohardagga, No. 11, Ranchi 22 May 1880, *PAC.*, i, p. 83.

44. Haldar, to D. C. Lohardagga, No. 11, Ranchi 22 May 1800, p. 83;

lands to which they had not any shadow of right." The landlords confounded the Christians with "agitators" and looked upon them as not only "unproductive *raiyats*" but also those who introduced into the village an element of opposition to their demands whether just or unjust.[45] During 1855-57 the zamindars, alarmed at the spread of Christianity in a bid to "terrorise not only the neophyts out of their allegiance to the German Mission but also the Missionaries out of Chotanagpur",[46] harassed the Christian *raiyats*. In 1855, a *thikadar* assaulted a Missionary Hortzog, beat him up mercilessly and left him almost dead. The culprit was fined.[47] In 1856, the zamindars cut the paddy of Christians in twenty villages, and those of 30 villages decided to drive out the missionaries. During the early phases of the Mutiny of 1857, the zamindars had the upper hand, and they came down upon the missionaries and the Christians who fomented agrarian discontent. They attacked the German Mission Church at Ranchi, took away what they found there, and destroyed a musical organ. The Christians in the villages were persecuted, they left their house and fled to the jungles; one or two of them hid themselves on an island in river Karo near Dukargari. Thakur Bishwanath Singh, a leader of the Mutiny at Ranchi, wrote to all his friend zamindars to put an end to the Christians, but the intervention of *Raja* of Chotanagpur saved the situation. Yet out of 56 villages, in only two Christians could remain safe,[48] and from others they were driven out by the zamindars who nullified the previous orders of the courts,[49] caused a wholesale spoliation of the property of the Christians, many of whom died of starvation in the jungles, although some were only saved by their non-Christian neighbours.[50] With the suppression of the Mutiny the tide turned. The Sardar Movement

45. Hunter, *op. cit.*, p 447.

46. H. Wueste, *Christian Church in Chotanagpur*, p. 28.

47. Hoflmann, *Epcyclopaedia Mudarica* viii, s. v. "*ghus*" pp. 1446-47

48. Haldar to D. C. Lohardagga No. 11, Ranchi 22 May 1880, *PAC.* i, p. 83.

49. *Ibid.*

50. M. G. Hallet, Bihar and Orissa District Gazetteers, Ranchi, Patna, 1917, p. 226.

from 1859 onwards marked the beginning of the offensive of Christian raiyats against the zamindars.

The Chotanagpur Encumbered Estates Act (Act VI of 1876) was intended to protect the old encumbered estates; it had as its object "the preservation of old families from ruin, and the maintenance of the ties, which exist between the old settlers and their hereditary chiefs."[51] The Commissioner, under the Act, could appoint a manager to look after the estates, which could not be sold in execution of any decree. It was 'undoubtedly a political necessity", and at a time of growing antagonism between the landlords and the *raiyats*, "transfer of old estates to aliens could hardly fail to be calamitous."[52] But the Act resulted in the forcible break-up of the *khuntkatti* system in Siri and Sonepur. In Siri when the Special Commissioner during the Bhuinhari survey held that the area was *khuntkatti* and "the *Majhias* lands could exist in it",[53] the zamindar applied for protection under the Act. The Estate was taken over, and the manager either through the "ignorance of the system of land tenure" or "a mistaken zeal for the estates under management,"[54] proceeded to destroy the *khuntkatti* system in the area and enlarge the area of *majhias* lands of landlords. Similarly in the Jaria Estate, when it was under the management of the Encumbered Estates Department, the *khuntkatti* system in its villages was "completely broken.[55] The *khuntkatti* lands were usurped and recorded as *rajhas*. The disqualified landlord further extended the area of *majhias* lands till he possessed such lands" in almost every village.[56] This example of the Encumbered Estates management must have been a powerful incentive to other landlords and they, no doubt, followed the example". No wonder at the time of the commencement of the settlement operations (1902-10)—the area under the *khuntkatti* system had "enormously contracted."[57]

The Chotanagpur Landlord and Tenant Procedure Act

51, J. Reid, *op. cit.*, p. 37.
52. *Ibid.*, p. 38.
53. *Ibid.*, p. 82.
54. *Ibid.*
55. *Ibid.*, p. 83.
56. *Ibid.*
57. *Ibid.*

(Act I of 1879), which sought to regulate the relations of landlords and tenants, was a half-hearted measure. Though based on Act I of 1859, it dropped the provisions about distraint and enhancement of rent. It weighed in favour of the landlords, for commutation of praedial conditions or services was optional. Enhancement of rent in respect of such lands as *bhuinhari*, *khuntkatti* and *korkar* was permissible only under certain conditions, and the restriction on the sale of under tenure for arrears of rent continued. The Act did not reflect the urgency of the situation and could hardly cope with the pressing agrarian issues of the period.

A redeeming feature of the eighties was the settlement of the Chotanagpur Estate (1877-1886), "exceedingly"[58] well done by Slacke. It covered an area of 742.00 square miles, excluding some rents of it.[59] It established agrarian peace in a large portion of territory in Chotanagpur. About 93 p.c. of the *raiyats* with a few exceptions accepted the settlement[60] and signed the rent roll. It was "fair to both parties, giving a moderately enhanced rent while abolishing all labour demands and cesses.[61] Though it did not have the sanction of law, the Raia was induced "to give receipts in accordance with the rent fixed by it."[62] This experiment was not extended to other parts of the district.

The five years preceding the Birsa movement (1895-(1900) were marked by fruitless deliberations on measures relating to forced labour and the praedial conditions and to the extension of the Bengal Tenancy Act to Chotanagpur. In 1890 several meetings were held in Ranchi to discuss the agrarian situation pertaining to the region away from the explosive "quadrilateral". On 15 March 1890 the Lieutenant Governor, the Commissioner, Grimley, A. Nottrott and P. Nolan, Secretary to the Government of Bengal, Revenue Department, met the Sardar and *raiyats* merely to hear the

58. C. C. Stevens, Commissioner of Chotanagpur Division to the Secretary to the Board of Revenue, Lower Provinces Rev,. Deptt., No. 99, Chotanagpur, 18 April 188.

59. *Ibid.*

60. Minutes of proceedings at a conference held at Ranchi on 18 March 1890, *PAC*, ii, pp. 43-45.

61. B. Nolan, to Commr. to Chotanagpur Division letter no 1258-491 L. R. dated Calcutta, 7 April 1890, *PAC*, ii, pp. 47 to 51.

62. *Ibid.*

latters' views.[63] Join Sardar complained that "the police and Zamindars had united to plunder the property of the *raiyats*", carried off to forced labour, "the favourite subjects of the Sardars." Asked whether they would give labour where it was legally due their reply implied that "in many cases in which it was demanded they would not give it." The majority of *raiyats* agreed to bear the cost of the settlement operations. A Sardar claimed that he was compelled to do forced labour by a zamindar in the face of a "High Court decree declaring him exempt from forced labour." Others mentioned their being "cheated of land at the *bhuinhari* settlement by collusion and false witnesses."[64] The same complaints were repeated on 17 March. The zamindars suggested survey and settlement operations in disturbed villages, recording of the existing rent, fixing a fair rent for every field[65]—a method found successful in Bengal and the Santhal Pargana, but the expense involved in it was prohibitive. In the alternative, an officer was to be deputed to merely "ascertain existing rents without measurements", but this was no lasting solution to the problem. Commutation of payment in kind into cash was desirable. The lacunae of the existing rent law were absence of "any of evidence for fixing fair rents." The extension of Bengal Tenancy Act to Chotanagpur was strongly advocated as it would legally facilitate a Survey and Settlement operation and "regulate the action of the court in fixing rents, and generally place the conduct of litigation of this class on a better basis."[66]

In the last conference held at Ranchi on 18 March 1890 attended by Revd. J. C. Whitley of S. P. C. Mission, F. Hahn of the G.E.L. Mission and Father Lievans of the R. C. Mission, G. T. Peppe, W. Maude and Babu Rai Charan Ghosh and Babu Devendra Lal Bose, representatives of the zamindars, the agrarian issue was discussed threadbare. It was "agreed generally" that an enquiry and settlement of disputes in some

63. Memorandum of a discussion with certain representatives ryot held on 15 March 1890. *Papers relating to Agrarian disputes in Chotanagpur*, Vol. ii, p. 39.

64. *Ibid.*

65. P. Nolan, Points for enquiry and discussion, 15 March 1900, *ibid.*

66. *Ibid.*

form or other were "necessary."[67] As regards the survey and settlement operations, the consensus was that the law might be framed so as to give the Lieutenant Governor the power either to make a regular settlement and survey or to make a local enquiry and record existing rents and rights. This was equally vague and totally inadequate to meet the urgency of the situation. The subject of commutation evoked different reactions. To Peppe, a representative of the Chotanagpur Estate, the enforcement of commutation of *beth begari* would be "odious to the people and objectionable to the zamindars", the first would react adversely because this would mean an addition to their actual money rent. He held that the agitation resulted not from dislike of forced labour but from the *raiyats* "having been worked upon by certain missionaries gentlemen with a view to gaining them over to their own church." It was suggested that the power to commute the service altogether should be given to it. Governor Rev. Hahn of the G.E.L. Mission was of the opinion that "*rakmats* were a constant source of annoyance and harrassment to the people, specially as they included certain cesses for religious purposes, which were distasteful to Christian converts." Sir John Edgar was doubtful whether "the cases could be converted without a survey of the district." The subject of extending the survey to the whole district was discussed but dropped. As regards the extension of the Bengal Tenancy Act to Chotanagpur, regulating the enhancement of rent, "the legal advisers of the zamindars were believed to be opposed to it, "though the Lt. Governor believed that it would be easier to extend the Act than to "introduce modifications into it" or "bring in a new bill altogether". Rev. Hahn approved of it and felt that "it would be favourable to the *raiyats* and the zamindars alike."[68]

The conference broke up without arriving at any conclusion. It highlighted the different facets of the agrarian problem, commutation of forced labour and praedial conditions, standard ren ı measurement, etc. But all hinged on a

67. Minutes of proceedings at a conference held at Ranchi on 18 March 1890, *ibid.*, pp. 41-44

68. *Ibid.* The introduction of a standard land measure in place of the indefinite measures in use "was dependent on a survey and settlement operation".

full-fledged survey and settlement operation, which alone could stabilise the agrarian situation. Secondly, the extension of the Bengal Tenancy Act or the framing of a new Act would alone make such a settlement operation possible. Although the necessity of the settlement operation was realised by all, its urgency was not felt. The Lt. Governor thought that the question of the cause of the dispute, though very important, could not be made a "subject for discussion" in conference. The Commissioner of Chotanagpur was to report "at the earliest possible date"[69] on the extension of the Bengal Tenancy Act to Chotanagpur in consultation with local authorities because the Lt. Governor did not find any tangible objection to it during the discussion at Ranchi. In 1890, the Commissioner submitted a report on the working of the Act 1 of 1879, in which he noted the absence of a definition of rent,[70] of a fixed unit or standard of measurement, of a definite standard of reference, of provision for deposit of rent and for bestowing the status of an occupancy *raiyat* on any holding land in any village, and of the extension of occupancy right to *bhuinhari* tenure not assessable to enhanced rent. He further recommended introduction of certain sections of Bengal Tenancy Act into Chotanagpur, particularly those of Chapter X relating to the preparation of a record of right and survey and settlement which would do "the greatest possible good to both landlords and tenants."[71] He also suggested that the Bengal Tenancy Act procedure regarding enhancement of rent be adopted.

The draft of a bill to regulate the procedure for the commutation of praedial conditions pertaining to lands in Chotanagpur was communicated to Government of India;[72] Chapter II of the bill was "appropriated *mutatis mutandis* from the Bengal Tenancy Act of 1885."[73] The Governor

69. *Ibid.*

70. W. H. Grimley, to Secy. to Govt. of Bengal, Rev. Deptt., No. 639J, Ranchi, 14 Nov. 1890, *Progs.* No. 24, June 1892, Rev. Deptt. "Extension of the Tenancy Act to the Chotanagpur Division", pp. 5-21.

71. *Ibid.*

72. S. H. Reley, Asstt. Secy. to Govt. of Bengal, Legislative Deptt. to Secy. to Govt. of Bengal, Rev. Deptt., No. 39/T, Calcutta the 17 Feb. 1891, *Progs*, No. 25, June 1892, Land-Revenue.

73. *Ibid.*

agreed that the extension of the Bengal Tenancy Act to Chotanagpur would legally authorise the Government to make formal records of rights in order to settle disputes.[74] The Government of India proposed some amendments to the substantive provisions of the Bill,[75] which was sent to the Commissioner of Chotanagpur for comment. In November 1892 Sir Charles Eliot visited Chotanagpur chiefly for the purpose of discussing the extension of the Bengal Tenancy Act to that Division and also the supplementary bill to regulate enhancement of rents and the commutation of praedial conditions[76] or services. He also addressed himself to three leading questions,[77] which had to be solved in order to obtain a satisfactory settlement of the relations between the landlord and the tenant in Chotanagpur. These related to securing "the grantor's right of resumption on the failure of male heirs", the settling of disputes about *rakumat* and *beth begari* by recording them or by "compulsory commutation", and, lastly, ascertaining the claim of landlords to enhancement of rent "on the ground of low rents or of the great privileges granted to tenants. The Commissioner was asked to call a conference of "persons representing the interests of landlords and tenants and to discuss with them certain points which require to be settled."[78] The conference was held in 1893-94, and the Bill was revised in the light of the suggestions made.[79] The Government of India returned the Bill regulating rent and commutation with its comments, and the Commissioner submitted his reply. It was still on the anvil when the Birsa movement broke out.

Although the first phase of the Birsa Movement in 1895 proved to be abortive, it led to "several immediate improvements of the law (not effective enough) in favour of the agricultural classes." The change of the attitude of the local Government "into one of distinct kindness to the Aborigines"

74. C. E. Buckland, Offg. Secy. to Govt. of Bengal, Rev. Deptt. to Secy. to Govt. of India, Rev. & Agr. Deptt. No. 547-L-R., Calcutta, 24 April 1891; *Progs.* No. 26, June 1892, Rev. Deptt., Land Revenue, pp. 22-25.

75. *Report on Administration of Bengal* 1895-96, p. 42.

76. *Ibid.*

77. *Ibid.*

78. *Ibid.*

79. *Ibid.*

was not quite perceptible. In day-to-day administrative matters the attitude of Col. Gordon's successor H. C. Streatffild might have done much "to dissipate the long standing diffidence"[80] (of the aboriginals), but it did not go far enough. During the period 1895 to 1899 the Government remained bogged down in discussions about suitable legislative measures. In 1894-95 the Bill to "regulate the enhancement of rent and commutation of praedial condition" was under consideration of the State Government in the light of the comments of the Government of India.[81] Subsequently a bill, amended in accordance with the suggestion of Government of India, was submitted during 1895-96. It was, however, actually introduced in the Bengal Legislative Council in 1897[82] "after several years of discussion." It provided for the voluntary commutation of praedial conditions and services, laid down an elaborate procedure for the enhancement of rent, and regulated "the registration and resumption of intermediate tenures." It came in for criticism by a certain group of persons, and the question of the extension of Bengal Tenancy Act to Chotanagpur was postponed. The Governor considered it "inadvisable to delay indefinitely the enactment of the provisions relating to commutation of praedial services and conditions."[83]

The Bill was, for the second time, accordingly modified, and became Act IV of 1897, or the Commutation Act. It empowered the Governor to compulsorily commutate praedial services and conditions when it was considered expedient to do so.[84] The Act, in practice, did not amount to any relief for a Munda; it proved to be merely palliative. In fact, nothing short of a record of rights and survey based on a thorough investigation of local customs in the matter could have made sense to the people and made such legislation effective. In its absence, the Act remained a dead letter; the Government did not exercise its special power.[85] Adminis-

80. Hoffmann, *Encyclopaedia Mundarica*, s.v. "Birsa Bhagoan", p. 570.
81. *Ibid.*
82. *Report on Administration of Bengal*, 1894.
83. *Ibid.*
84. Reid, *op. cit.*, p. 43.
85. *Ibid.*

tratively, the Act was a fiasco. The *raiyats*, who were on good terms with their landlords, had no objection whatsoever to meeting a portion of their rent in the shape of physical labour. The Christian *raiyat* would not just pay. The landlords would claim that their demand was "limited only by their requirements" and nothing more. Further, the costs of litigation were "phenomenal". There were minor deterrents too; cases of "miscarriage of justice in a few cases," and allowing "money payment in lieu of services" which were "sometimes greatly in excess of the scale laid down by Grimley". Thus the "operation of the Act" was a "failure", and it did not exercise any "appreciable influence as a solution of agrarian trouble."[86] It only made the compelling necessity of a survey and settlement operation clear.

The Act did not evoke any enthusiasm among the Mundas.[87] The Sardars were out to wreck it. They engaged their unfailing friend and counsel, Jacob; but the suggestions offered by him during the preparation of the Bill were ignored. The Act, when passed, "gave any thing but satisfaction to the tenants", and Jacob was obliged to advise them to "ignore it." A large number of cases were filed "with the avowed object of proving that it was perfectly useless and unworkable." On the assurance of the authorities that "the law" would be "altered," Jacob on behalf of the tenants, "agreed to hold over the cases under the Commutation Act."[88]

As regards the more important question of the extension of the Bengal Tenancy Act and of the resumption and restoration of tenures, it was referred to the Board of Revenue. The Commissioner finally "proposed a bill to amend the several enactments relating to the law of landlord and tenant"[89] in the division. The Bill was considered in 1899, when in view of the Birsa movement of 1895 and the continuing "acute agrarian unrest" he considered this measure to be "inadvisable and inopportune", because "the discussions might lead to

86. Reid, *op. cit.*, p. 44.

87. The *Charbandhu* of 1 Feb. 1897 came out with a cryptic note on the provisions of the Act.

88. "The case of the Mundas", *Calcutta Review*, Vol. 1. 10, 1900, pp. 357-64.

89. Reid, *op. cit.*, p. 43.

further excitement among an already excited and credulous people."[90] The whole thing was to wait till a survey and settlement operation would bring to light relevant data.

Agrarian movements :

The Sardar movement or *Mulkui larai* (the struggle for the land), which lasted for fifty years (1859 to 1908), was basically agrarian. The Sardars (Oraon and Munda) were stimulated by concept of the Golden Age when there were no Rajas and Zamindars. As descendants of the original settlers, they insisted on the restoration of the land they or their ancestors had always held possession of (later Sardars insisted on the restoration of their lands they had been tricked into giving away at the time of the Bhuinhari Settlement, 1869-81). They raised their voice against the multiplying incidences of rents, praedial conditions and *beth begari* (forced labour), called for the expulsion of *dikus*, middlemen and zamindars, and pleaded that they be taken under the direct administration of the British. They laid stress, under the influence of the German missionaries, on the restoration of peasant proprietorship as prevalent in the German states, rather than on the semi-communal character of the *khuntkatti* system. The movement embraced both Oraons and Mundas. Most of the Sardars relied on prayer, protest and petition to achieve their objectives, on placing petitions before the local authorities, the Viceroy, the Queen and the Parliament, and on fighting their imaginary cases in the courts. The tribals were made to believe that the Governor-General and Viceroy, i.e., the great *Sarkar*, was on the side of the agitators, but that the local authorities of Ranchi were supporting the zamindars and moneylenders. Thus started the Mundas' distrust of the local authorities.

The Sardar movement passed through three phases: the agrarian phase (1858-1881), the revivalistic phase (1881-90) and the political phase (1890-91); and finally it culminated into a politico-religious movement under Birsa. The agrarian question remained the propelling force behind the Sardar movement throughout the period. The Birsa movement (1895-1900) only tried to attain Sardars' agrarian objectives

90 *bid.*, p. 44.

in a larger political and religious context by founding a Munda Raj and Munda religion. Birsa borrowed the entire gamut of Sardars' agrarian ideas : The Mundas were true owners of the soil; they had appointed the Maharaja, rent was paid to him towards his maintenance and not in acknowledgement of his rights in the land.

The land revenue administration and legislation.

After the Birsa movement, the violent agitation among the Mundas "entirely died away", but the "feelings which gave rise to it "smouldered" as widely as ever.[91] The relations between landlords and *raiyats* were as "unsatisfactory" as could be; while the former held that the latter existed for "their own use and convenience", the latter claimed to be "genuine owners of the soil."[92] An immediate result of the uprising was the authorities' awareness of the urgency of preparing a record of rights for the lands of discontented Mundas. More than any other movement in the 19th century, the Birsa uprising jolted them into a clear perception of the issues involved; what the Mundas needed was security of their tenure, recognition of their rights in land and the preservation of the Mundari *khuntkatti* system. Only a settlement operation could provide the basis of agrarian security, bring to light the variety of local customs and tenures, determine them with precision and secure them. In the past a settlement operation had been considered too costly a proposition. The *bhuinhari* Settlement operation (1869-80) was limited in its scope. In the absence of a settlement even well-meant measures such as the Commutation Act of 1897 were infructuous. Sir John Woodburn, the Lieutenant Governor of Bengal, however, entertained doubts about the advisability of a general settlement; he apprehended that the general excitement and animosities "between *raiyats* and zamindars" arising out of a general survey might lead to a "fresh outbreak". The Jesuit father,[93] Rev. Hoffmann, assured the authorities that "there would not only be no danger of new rising" and

91. Report of Streatfeild, D. C., Miscellaneous Report of the Chotanagpur Division for 1900-1901, *Progs.* Nos. 1-6, Nov., Misc. Gen. Deptt., Govt. of Bengal, p. 7.

92. *Ibid.*, p. 9

93. Hoffmann, *Encyclopaedia Mundarica*, ii, s. v. "Birsa Bhagoan", pp. 57-71.

that "the cultivators themselves desired a settlement" as the only means to put a stop to further aggressions from the zamindars, and give them "that feeling of security they stood so much in need of after long years of constant anxiety".[94] In refereshing contrast to the ignorance, if not apathy, of the earlier administrators the Commissioner, A. Forbes, strongly felt that the troubles would continue till "a complete survey and record of rights" was prepared "throughout the Munda country" and also the *beth begari* system" was "abolished."[95]

The earlier *bhuinhari* settlement in 1869 did not extend over the Munda areas of Khunti, Tamar, Bundu and Sonahatu police stations, the centre of Birsa's movement. As the new settlement operations commenced in these police stations, the Mundas warmly welcomed them.[96] When the Governor visited Ranchi in February 1904, he received an address from various classes of population urging the "extension of the operation,"[97] which was done.

The Settlement operations, judged by their results, resembled "a calm, sunny morning after a long destructive hurricane which had reduced the Mundas to extreme poverty and had thrown hundreds of thousands for ever far away from their own country."[98] It brought "peace and security"[99] to those that remained. There has been no recurrence of the agrarian trouble of the magnitude of the last century; the Sardar agitation died down, though the "petition mongering" continues till to-day. It restored a feeling of confidence among the aboriginals, made the authorities aware of the implications of their land system and of the need to safeguard their rights. It led to the compulsory commutation of praedial conditions, their abolition and also that of the *beth begari* system, the "secondary cases of dispute" were now "finally set at rest."[100] The Commutation Act of 1897 was a failure and had not pro-

94. *Ibid.*

95. Quoted in J. Reid, *Final Report on the Survey and Settlement Operations in Ranchi*, 1902-10, pp. 46-47.

96. *Ibid.*

97. *Ibid.*

98. Hoffmann, *Encyclopaedia Mundarica*, viii, s. v. "*Khuntkatti*", pp. 2402-04.

99. *Ibid.*

100. Reid, *op. cit.*, p. 34.

vided a "solution of (the) agrarian trouble".[101] Further, the "obligatory nature of all usury loan acknowledgements into usufructuary ones" and their repayment by means of Government loans at easy interest, to some extent freed the Munda peasant from "the inextricable meshes of the heartless usurers."[102] An index of the changed and peaceful times was the fall in the number of cases, civil and criminal, the latter being mostly cases of paddy theft and trespass which plagued the late eighties. In courts at Gumla and Khunti "the number of title suits fell from 137 and 244 in 1907 to 62 and 70 in 1910, respectively";[103] the "average number of suits filed annually during the last four years" was 72 at Gumla and 74 at Khunti. Suits for arrears of rent could be relatively easily disposed of at "a single hearing" on the production of the rent receipt which the landlords no longer withheld from their tenants. Litigation ceased to be a gamble.[104]

At the instance of the Lieutenant Governor of Bengal, Father Hoffmann, the most eminent missionary in the area, prepared a full description of the Munda land system to be appended to the forthcoming Act to enable the officials to understand it. The Memorandum on the Mundari *khuntkatti* system submitted by him and E. Lister was a valuable treatise; it was the first recognition, both official and non-official, of the system.

The settlement operations brought to light a mass of facts which made possible an "emergent legislation."[105] In 1899 in view of the ferment in the Munda country the "proposed bill to consolidate the law of landlords and tenants" had been postponed.[106] The Tenancy Amendment Act of 1903 was the first legal recognition of the Mundari *khuntkatti* system, the precursor of subsequent Act of 1908. It stopped all forms of mortagage except that known as *Bhugutt bandh*, recognised the custom and allowed certain forms of transfer to

101. *Ibid.*, p. 44.

102. Hoffmann, *Encyclopaedia Mundarica*, viii, s.v.'*Khuntkatti*", pp. 2402-2404.

103. Hallett, *Bihar & Orissa Dist. Gazetteers, Ranchi*, pp. 52-35.

104. *Ibid.*

105. Reid, op. cit., p. 48.

106. *Ibid.*

other Mundaris, invested the Deputy Commissioner with powers to give effect to the prohibition of sale and certain restrictions on transfer, provided for realisation of arrears of rent, and secured finality of the record-of-rights. At the instigation of the Sardars if the members of the brotherhood refused to pay any rent, their tenancy was sold up. Now the Settlement Officer could not only give security to members of a Mundari *khuntkatti* brotherhood in an intact *khuntkatti* village but also afford them protection from further "molestation."[107]

The settlement operations made it clear that the agrarian law of Chhotanagpur needed "thorough revision" and preparation of a more comprehensive legal enactment. The existing Tenancy Act did not take into account, in several "important respects", the rights enjoyed by the aboriginal cultivators. A rough draft of a revised Bill was prepared, and its provisions were discussed in detail during the visit of Sir Andrew to Ranchi in August 1907, and in many conferences attended by the officers, landlords and tenants of Chotanagpur, "practical unanimity was obtained regarding most of the matters dealt with in the revised Bill." The Bill was subsequently introduced in the Council and passed as the Chotanagpur Tenancy Act VI of 1908.

The Chotanagpur Tenancy Act of 1908 marked the end of a century of agararian strife and was a measure of capital significance. It was the culmination of the legal and administrative measures taken so far to remove the agrarian discontent; the Chotanagpur Tenure Act of 1869, the Chotanagpur Landlord and Tenants Procedure Act of 1879, and finally the Commutation Act of 1897 were stepping stones to it. Its objects were to "supersede and consolidate the Acts in force in the division, to improve and amplify the procedure and to improve and complete the substantive law by embodying in it certain provisions of the Bengal Tenancy Act and some additional provisions "which affirmed" Kols' customary rights and usages."[108] The terms *khuntkattidar* and Mundari *khuntkattidar* tenancy were defined. The Act "safeguarded a number of points", which the Mundas claimed "as a central part of

107. Hoffmann, *Encyclopaedia Mundarica*, viii, p. 2387.

108. Reid, *Chotanagpur Tenancy Act*, *Act VI of* 1908.

their social system.[109] Since the land within the boundaries of the village was considered to be the common property of the village family and since members of the village family were thought to be direct descendants of the original founder[110] of the village, no individual could alienate his land. The Deputy Commissioner was empowered to eject forcibly any alien who may have acquired lands in the *khuntkattidar* village. There are restrictions on the sale and transfer of tribal lands and provisions for grant of rent receipts and commutation of rent, etc. These constituted the "most important and effective part of the legislation undertaken in favour of Mundari *khuntkattidars*."[111]

The *buinhars* and *khuntkattidars* are now settled *raiyats* in certain cases and enjoy occupancy rights (Sections 18-19). The most important sections are termed special provisions with respect to the Mundari *khuntkattidars* (Chapter 18). Important provisions relate to restrictions on transfer of the Mundari *khuntkatti* tenancies (Section 240), ejectment of persons unlawfully obtaining possession of such tenancies (242), etc. These sections have fortified the existing Mundari *khuntkatti* tenancies. Sections 46, 47 and 48 deal with restrictions on transfer of rights by *raiyats*, or sale of *raiyat's* right in pursuance of Court's order, or transfer or sale of *bhuinhari* tenures. A cause of grievance of the people against zamindars in respect of payment of rents was removed by provisions under Sections 53, 54, 55 and 56 of the Act. Grant of receipt for rent, which was seldom the practice earlier, and provision for deposit of rent in the Court of the Deputy Commissioner, constituted important safeguards against the vagaries of the *jagirdars*. The traditional tribal right to convert the land into *kokar* was recognised (Sec. 64) ; the Munda custom that those who reclaimed the land owned it was secured. The praedial conditions lay at the root of the agrarian strife; their commutation, was provided for (Chapter 13). The non-recognition of the rights of the Mundas that underlay the agrarian strife of the last century was thus largely remedied.

However, so far as the safeguard of *khuntkatti* rights was concerned, the Act came rather late for more than "nine-

109. Hoffmann, *Encyclopaedia Mundarica*, viii, pp. 2382-83.
110. *Ibid.*
111. *Ibid.*

tenths of the race."[112] Only 156 villages could be secured as intact Mundari *khuntkatti* villages. The Act and the results of the survey fell short of some expectations of the Mundas ; many points of leakage remained; moneylenders continued as active as ever. But the Act made possible the following years of relative agrarian calm. The privileges then granted to the Mundas were "far greater than anything granted to any other class of Indian cultivators."[113]

The foregoing study describes the disintegration of the tribal agrarian system in Chotanagpur. The land revenue policy followed by the British Government betrayed ignorance of the tribal agrarian system and a hesitation to take prompt remedial action. Piecemeal legislations did not go far. The authorities tried with little success and much less beneficial results to strike a balance between zamindars' and *raiyats'* interests, creating the impression among the latter that the Government sought more to safeguard the rights and privileges of the former. This led to tribals' protest, legal and constitutional in the beginning and violent in the end, which is echoed to this day in their folksongs.

112. *Ibid.*
113. *Ibid.*

GLOSSARY

bali	petty cess (*AŚ*); emergency tax (*Milinda-pañho*); the same as *bhāga* (inscriptions & law-books)
barqandāz	a matchlockman, guard, or escort
baṭaī	sharing the produce of land by division; (a sub-division of the *ghalla-bakhshī* system, vide below)
baṭṭā	discount
begār	forced labour
bethbegārī	begār-forced labour for which no pay was given
bhāga	king's customary share of the produce, usually amounting to 1/6th
bhandari dhān	bhandaṛ—villages managed by the raja or zamindar himself, not rented or farmed to others
bhatta	allowance
bhogapati	revenue officer
bhoga	periodical supplies
bhuinhars	original clearers of lands among the Oraons and Mundas who provided the leadership during the rising
bighā	the standard unit of area; its actual size varied sharply from place to place and during different periods
Bir Kandar Disum	the valleys of Kanchi and Karkari rivers where the Khuntkatti system survives intact
chandā	subscription
cira-khila	land never brought under cultivation
daur panche	contribution made by a raiyat cultivating daur
dārogha	head of a police, custom or excise station
dasai	payment to the landlord at the time of Dasahara
dastūrs	schedules of assessment rate stated in cash

dastūru'l 'amal	administration manuals
dhānya	general land tax
dikus	non-tribal people
ditya	denoted all taxes except forced labour
diwān	a minister, a chief officer of an estate
foṭadārs	treasurers
qabẓ	security
gaz	yard
ghalla bakhshī	a system of assessment and collection of land evenue based on the division of the crop
ghaṭwālī-paikan	a land grant to the ghatwal (a tribal constable in the jungle Mahāls)
ghatwāls	marcher lords—paiks
gocara	tax on pastures
gopa	officer in charge of five or ten villages (*AŚ*, II, 35)
gumāshtās	clerks, subordinate officials
halikākara	plough tax (?)
ḥaqq-i-milkiat	right of ownership
har	plough
hast-o-būd	literal meaning 'is and was'; a summary form of assessment based on a rough surmise
hiraṇya	tax levied on commercial crops
ijāra	farming of revenue; contract
ilaqa'dār	the person who engages, either on his own account or as the representative of others, for the payment of the assessed revenue upon a district or a village
iqṭa'	an assignment of revenue; during the Sultanat period, it also meant a territorial unit. It became obsolete during the Mughal period and was replaced by 'jāgīr'.
jāgīr	a conditional or unconditional assignment of land or its revenue
jāgīrdār	holder of a jāgīr
jama'	state demand; valuation; credit
jama'-i-raqamī	statistics for the general assessment, as it existed under Sher Shah and early reign of Akbar

jarīb	a land measure, also the instrument of measurement
kankūt	a system of assessment of land revenue
karc	share due to the king and payable by one who enjoys the fruits of royal agricultural lands and pastures; dues paid by cultivators during the harvesting season; probably also some kind of oppressive impost
karpāsa	cotton growing trees
khalabhikṣā	beggings from the threshing floor
kharāj	technically, the tax imposed in Islamic kingdoms on the non-Muslims; generally used for state demand
khaliṣa	lands under the direct management of state, as opposed to lands whose revenue was assigned to individuals
kharposh (*khorposh*)	maintenance (grants)
khila	fallow land
khorposhdārs	maintenance grantees
khud kāshta	land cultivated by the assignee directly
khunlkaṭṭīdār	original clearers of land in Chota-Nagpur proper
khuṭ	collector of revenue; also used for minor Hindu chiefs or inter mediary
kili	clan
kori	digging
kaṭnī	cutting
madad ma'āsh	grant of land for subsistence
mahto	a village headman among the Oraons
māngan	gift
mankī	a circle headman among the Mundas
meya	probably a substitute for *bhāga*
misri	thrashing
morabandhi	storing the grain
muqarraridār	a person holding land at a fixed rate of assessment
mundā	a village headman among the Mundas
muqṭa'ī	a form of assessment, generally indicating payment of a fixed amount; controversy about its exact meaning

maqṭa'	provincial governors, used in this sense during Sultanat period
nābūd	destroyed, ruined
nāla bhūmi	cultivable land
nasaq	a system of assessment of land revenue; the authorities differ about its exact meaning.
nayal	plough
nazrāna	a present
neg	customary payment on marriage
pāhan	the religious head of a Munda village
parganā	an administrative division
parhā	A group of Munda villages
paṭṭā	a deed of lease
patti	a half, a moiety
piṇḍakara	lump assessment on the entire village (*AŚ*, II, 15)
prītibhoga	daily presents in the form of fruits
rai'	revenue demand stated in grain; introduced by Sher Shah and continued in the early years of Akbar's reign
rājadeyavibhāga	(Caulukya) dues payable to the king
rautiā	horse soldier
ropini	sowing
salāmī	a complimentary present
śaṣyanidānibhūta dānī samvandhe	royal share that was to be deducted from the grain produced
sardār ghāṭwāl	chief ghatwal
sasān	the burial ground
ṣaṣṭhādhikṛta	land revenue officer
sharishtadār	record-keeper
suḍs	foreigners
suka-dhānya	spring crops, e.g., wheat, barley, etc.
suyūrghāl	grant by emperors of either a cash allowance or a jāgīr
tabe'dār	subordinate
taḥqīq	verification, research
tahṣīldār	a native collector of revenue
ṭanāb	instrument of measurement; rope
taqāvī	literal meaning 'giving strength'; aid to cultivators

ṭaraf	*jāgīr*
thikadār	farmer of revenue or excise
tiyūl	an assignment of revenue such as *jāgīr*, *iqṭa'*
udakabhāga	irrigation tax (*AŚ*)
udraṅga	a levy over and above the usual grain share
uparikara	an extra cess, but actual nature undefined
ẓabṭ	a system of assessment based on measurement and fixing of *rai'*

BIBLIOGRAPHY

I Primary and Secondary Sources

Āīn-i-Akbarī of Abul Fazl — Eng. Tr. by Blochmann and J. S. Jarrett, Calcutta, 1873

Amarakośa of Amara Siṁha (with the commentary of Ksīrasvāmī) — Ed. by H. D. Sharma and G. N. Sardesai, Poona, 1941.

Arthaśāstra of Kauṭilya — Ed. by R. Shama Sastry, 3rd Edn., Mysore, 1924. Eng. Tr. by R. Shama Sastry, 7th edn., Mysore, 1961, Ed. with Commentary by T. Ganapati Sastri, 3 Vols. Trivandrum, 1924-25.

Bṛhaspatismṛti — Reconstructed by K. V. R. Aiyangar GOS, Baroda, 1941, Eng. Tr. by J. Jolly, SBE, Oxford, 1881.

Buddhacarita of Aśvaghoṣa — Ed. and Tr. by E. H. Johnston (Punjab University Oriental Publication No. 31), Lahore, 1935.

Jātakamālā of Āryasūra — Ed. by H. Kern, Boston, 1871. Eng. Tr. by J. Speyer, London 1895.

Kṛtyakalpataru, (*Rājadharmakāṇḍa*), of Laksmidhara — Ed. by K. V. Rangaswami Aiyangar Gaekwad Oriental Series, No. C Baroda, 1943.

Lekhapaddhati — Ed. by C. D. Dalal & Shrigaonkar Gaikwar Oriental Series, XIX, 1925.

Mahāvaṁśa — Ed. by W. Geiger, PTS, London, 1908. Eng. Tr. by W. Geiger (The Great Chronicles of Ceylon), London, 1912.

Mānava Dharmasūtra or *Manusmṛti* — Ed. by J. Jolly, London, 1887 Eng. Tr. by G. Bühler, SBE, Oxford, 1886. Eng. Tr. by G. Jha, 5 Vols. Calcutta, 1922-29

Milindapañho — Ed. by V. Trenckner, London, 1880. Eng. Tr. by T.W. Rhys Davids, SBE, Oxford, 1890-94.

Nāradasmṛti — Ed. by J. Jolly, Calcutta, 1885, Eng.

Tr. by J. Jolly, SBE, XXXIII, Oxford, 1889.

Prabandhacintāmaṇi of Merutuṅga — Ed. by Jinavijaya Muni, Santiniketan, 1933.

Raghuvaṁśa of Kālidāsa — Nirnayasagar Press, Bombay, 1929.

Rājanītiprakāśa — Chowkhamba Sanskrit Series.

Rājanītiratnākara of Caṇḍeśvara — Ed. by K. P Jayaswal

Rājataraṅginī of Kalhaṇa — Ed by M. Aurel Stein, Bombay, 1892 Eng. Tr. by M. A. Stein, London, 1900.

Śāntiparva of the *Mahābhārata* — Critical edition by S. K. Belvalkar, Poona, 1949-54. Eng. Tr. by K. M. Ganguly, Published by P. C. Roy, Calcutta, 1884-96.

Saundarananda Kāvya of Aśvaghoṣa — Ed. by E. H. Johnston, London, 1928. English Translation by E. H. Johnston, 2 Vols., London 1932.

Viṣṇusmṛti — Ed. by J. Jolly, Calcutta, 1881. Eng. Tr. by J. Jolly, SBE, VII, Oxford, 1880.

Altekar, A. S. — *Rāṣṭrakuṭas and Their Times*, Poona, 1934.

Baden Powell — *The Land System of British India*, Oxford, 1891.

Bandopadhyaya, N.C. — *Kauṭilya*, Calcutta, 1927.

Bannerjee, D. N. — *Early Land Revenue System in Bengal and Bihar*, I, Calcutta, 1936.

Bradley Birt, E.B. — *Chotanagpur, a little known province of the Empire*, London, 1919.

Burns, Richard (ed.) — *Cambridge History of India*, IV, Cambridge, 1963.

Chappot, Victor — *The Roman World*, London, 1928 (tr. from the Original French by E. A. Parker).

Dalton, E. T. — *Descriptive Ethnology of Bengal*, Calcutta, 1872.

Dodwell, H.H. (ed.) — *Cambridge History of India*, V, Delhi, 1963.

Elliot, H. M. and Dowson, John (ed.) — *History of India as told by its own Historians*, I, London, 1867-77.

Firminger, W. K. (ed.) — *The Fifth Report to the House of Commons on East India Affairs*, I, Calcutta, 1917-18.

Foster, W. — *Early Travel in India*, London, 1927.

Ghoshal, U. N. — *Contributions to the History of Hindu Revenue System*, Calcutta, 1929.

Guha, A. C. — *A Brief Sketch of Land System of Bengal and Bihar*, Calcutta, 1915.

Guha, Ranjit — *A Rule of Property for Bengal*, The Hague 1963.

Habib, Irfan — *The Agrarian System of Mughal India*, Bombay, 1963.

Hallet, M. G. — *Bihar and Orissa District Gazetteers*, Ranchi, Patna, 1917.

Hand, J. Reginald — *Early English Administration of Bihar* (1781-85), Calcutta, 1897.

Harrington, J. H. — *An Elementary Analysis of the Laws and Regulations enacted by the Governor-General in Council at Fort William*, III, Calcutta, 1805-22.

Hoffmann, Rev. — *Encyclopaedia Mundarica*, III, Calcutta, 1912.

Hunter, W. W. — *Our Indian Mussalmans*, London 1871.

Jha, G. N. — *Notes on Manusmṛti*, 3 Vols., Calcutta, 1924-29.

Jha, J. C. — *The Kol Insurrection in Chotanagpur*, Calcutta, 1964.

Hunter, W. W. (ed.) — *Bengal MS. Records* (1782-1807), I, London, 1894.

Macdonell, A. A., and Keith, A. B. — *Vedic Index of Names and Subjects*, 2 Vols., London, 1912.

McCrindle, J. W. — *Ancient India as described in Classical Literature*, Westminster, 1901.

Maity, S. K. — *Economic Life of Northern India in the Gupta Period*, Calcutta 1957.

Majumdar, Asoka — *Caulukyas of Gujarat*, Bombay, 1956.

Majumdar, B. P. — *Socio-Economic History of Northern India*, Calcutta, 1960.

Majumdar, R. C. — *History of Bengal*, Vol. I, Dacca, 1943.

Mill, J. — *History of British India*, IX London, 1826-35.

Misra, B. B. — *The Central Administration of the East India Company*, Manchester, 1959.

Moreland, W. H. — *The Agrarian System of Moslem India*, Cambridge, 1929.

Mukherjee, Radha Kamal — *Land Problems of India*, London, 1833.

Niyogi, Pushpa — *Contributions to the Economic History of Northern India*, Calcutta, 1962.

O'Malley, L.S.S. — *District Gazetteer*, Singhbhum Calcutta, 1910.

District Gazetteer, Manbhum, Calcutta, 1911.

District Gazetteer. Midnapore, Calcutta, 1911.

Rajaguru, S. N. — *Inscriptions of Orissa*, II

Ramsbotham, R. B. — *Studies in Land Revenue History of Bengal* (1769-87), London, 1926.

Reid, J. — *Final Report on the Survey and Settlement Operations in Ranchi*, 1902-10.

Ranchi Settlement Report (1902-1910), Calcutta, 1912.

————, *Final Report on Survey and Settlement Operations in the* Districts of Ranchi (1902-10), Calcutta, 1912.

Roy, S. C. — *Mundas and their Country*

Shamasastry — *Arthaśāstra* (tr.) Seventh edition Mysore, 1961.

Saran, P. — *The Provincial Government of the Mughals*, Allahabad, 1941.

Sharma, R. S. — *Aspects of Political Ideas and Institutions in Ancient India*, Delhi, 1959.

———— *Indian Feudalism* (300-1200), Calcutta, 1965.

———— *Light on Early Indian Society and Economy*, Bombay, 1966.

Sircar, D. C. — *Select Inscriptions Bearing on Indian History and Civilization*, I, Calcutta, 1942.

Watters, T. — *On Yuan Chwang's Travels In India*, I, 2 Vols., London, 1904-05.

Wueste, H. — *Christian Church in Chotanagpur*.

II Journals, Proceedings, etc.

Calcutta Review

Corpus Inscriptionum Indicarum

Epigraphia Indica

Indian Antiquary
Inscriptions of Bengal
Indian Historical Quarterly
Journal of Asiatic Society of Bengal
Journal of Bihar Research Society
Journal of Bihar and Orissa Research Society
Journal of the Bombay Branch of Royal Asiatic Society
Journal of Pakistan Historical Society
Journal of Royal Asiatic Society
Man In India
Proceedings of Indian History Congress
Proceedings of the Fourth Oriental Conference

INDEX